STAR WARS INSIDER PRESENTS

THE DARK SIDE COLLECTION

WELCOME...

Everybody loves a bad guy. While it's true to say that the heroes of the *Star Wars* saga are very popular, it's the villains who we are really waiting to see.

Star Wars has some of the best villains of all time, and none are better at being really bad than those most atuned to the dark side of the Force — the Sith. From visually arresting villains such as Darth Vader and Darth Maul to the slightly more subtle masters of evil like Darth Sidious and Count Dooku, we love to see these individuals give our protagonists a hard time and make their heroes' journey as difficult as possible.

This compendium of collected features offers a safe look at all things dark side, including interviews with the actors who brought some of the most iconic Sith Lords to life. There's also some expert analysis of the Sith's plans, motivations and how they fight for their sinister beliefs.

It's not all about the Sith Lords though. The dark side casts a long shadow and ambitious Force users Asajj Ventress and Kylo Ren are also profiled with detailed features and comments from the people who helped create these vivid, iconic characters.

Ultimately, this volume is a tribute to the talented creators of the *Star Wars* saga who have brought our darkest fears to life. Their hard work and dedication has resulted in some of our greatest nightmares and most compelling characters in pop culture history.

Jonathan

Jonathan Wilkins
Editor

TITAN EDITORIAL
Editor / Jonathan Wilkins
Group Editor / Jake Devine
Editorial Assistant / Ibraheem Kazi
Art Director / Oz Browne
Designer / David Colderley

LUCASFILM
Senior Editor / Brett Rector
Art Director / Troy Alders
Creative Director / Michael Siglain
Asset Management /
Chris Argyropoulos, Gabrielle Levenson,
Shahana Alam, Jackey Cabrera,
Elinor De La Torre, Bryce Pinkos,
Michael Trobiani, Sarah Williams
Story Group / Leland Chee, Pablo Hidalgo,
Emily Shkoukani, Phil Szostak,
and Kate Izquierdo

CONTRIBUTORS
Tricia Barr, Ben Grossblatt, Michael Kogge,
Megan Crouse, Bryan Cairns, Mark Wright,
Calum Waddell, Mark Newbold, Bryan Young,
Brett Rector

SPECIAL THANKS TO
Lucy Goldsmith, Erich Schoeneweiss
at Random House, Holly McIntosh,
Joseph Taraborrelli, Andrea Towers and
Jim Nausedas at Marvel Comics, Lizzy Draeger,
Tracy Cannobbio and Lyn Cowen at Lucasfilm.
Kevin P. Pearl, Samantha Keane,
and Eugene Paraszczuk at Disney.

TITAN MAGAZINES
Production Controllers /
Caterina Falqui & Kelly Fenton
Production Manager / Jackie Flook
Sales & Circulation Manager / Steve Tothill
Marketing Coordinator / Lauren Noding
Publicity & Sales Coordinator / Alexandra Iciek
Publicity Manager / Will O'Mullane
Publicist / Caitlin Storer
Digital & Marketing Manager / Jo Teather
Head of Creative & Business Development /
Duncan Baizley
Publishing Directors Ricky Claydon
& John Dziewiatkowski

Chief Operating Officer / Andrew Sumner
Publishers / Vivian Cheung & Nick Landau

DISTRIBUTION
U.S. Distribution / Penguin Random House
U.K. Distribution / MacMillon Distribution
Direct Sales Market / Diamond Comic
Distributors
General Enquiries / customerservice@
titanpublishingusa.com

Star Wars Insider Presents
The Dark Side Collection is published by Titan Magazines, a
division of Titan Publishing Group Limited, 144 Southwark
Street, London, SE1 0UP

Printed in China.
For sale in the U.S., Canada, U.K., and Eire

ISBN: 9781787744516

Contents

THE MAN BEHIND THE MASK

ULTIMATE STAR WARS CO-AUTHOR TRICIA BARR BRAVELY TAKES A PEEK INSIDE DARTH VADER'S HEAD.

Darth Vader intimidates me, now more than ever. Not in the way he terrified me as child, who was awed watching a black-clad, masked behemoth crush a windpipe with a single hand, then later with merely a thought. Today Vader casts a massive shadow across the panorama of modern mythology, a daunting prospect both for storytellers and those analyzing his impact. How does one begin to do justice to this iconic character's legacy? In a series of articles for *Star Wars Insider*, I have examined some of *Star Wars'* most notable heroes, their personal journeys through the saga, and what they have come to represent to the fans. We, too, take journeys with our fictional heroes, and find courage and inspiration in them. When confronting Darth Vader, I pondered what it is that we gain from our villains. The answer, in the end, is the same: Villains show us the truth of who we are.

THE MONSTER IN OUR HEADS

With Darth Vader's profound impression on the public consciousness, it is impossible to define his influence on everyone. To those who first met Vader in the prequel trilogy, he is a hero fallen. To my niece and nephews, Anakin Skywalker is the "Jedi With No Fear" from *Star Wars: The Clone Wars*—and Darth Vader is the bad guy at Disney Parks' Jedi Training Academy they must rally courage to defeat. I met Vader in 1977, when he marched through a bulkhead, dark and foreboding, and stalked down the white corridors of the *Tantive IV* with unrelenting focus on obtaining his objective. In that moment, my eight-year-old self was very afraid.

Our collective perception of Darth Vader has always been a collaborative phenomenon. In the book *The Complete Vader*, Ryder Windham relays an interview in which George Lucas describes how the characters Luke Skywalker and Darth Vader in *A New Hope* came from "one composite—which is saying they came out of me. I was dealing with two opposites, and these are the two opposites of myself." A rough draft summary dated May 1974 includes two separate villains: General Darth Vader, "a tall, grim-looking" humanoid, and Prince Valorum, a "black knight of the Sith... a sinister warrior in black robes and a face mask." The story continued to evolve with ideas and input from artist Ralph McQuarrie, sculptor Brian Muir, and other production staff helping to mold Darth Vader into his now-familiar character.

> "TWO METERS TALL. BIPEDAL. FLOWING BLACK ROBES TRAILING FROM THE FIGURE AND A FACE FOREVER MASKED BY A FUNCTIONAL IF BIZARRE BLACK METAL BREATH SCREEN—A DARK LORD OF THE SITH WAS AN AWESOME, THREATENING SHAPE AS IT STRODE THROUGH THE CORRIDORS OF THE REBEL SHIP."
> —STAR WARS NOVELIZATION (1976)

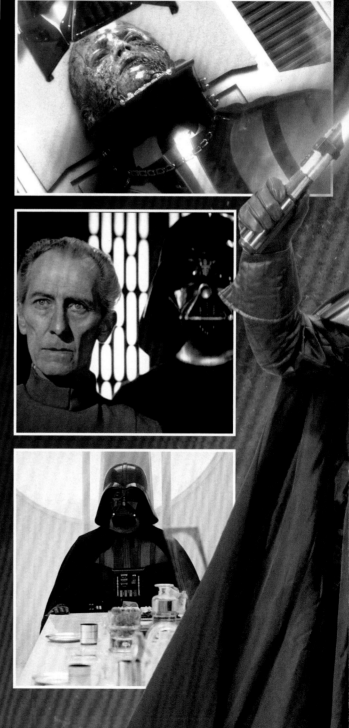

Many fans were introduced to the character prior to the film's release by way of the novelization, comics, and movie promotion. The 34th World Science Fiction Convention held in Kansas City, September 1976, included a special room dedicated to *Star Wars*, which featured the villain's costume. Long term fan Maggie Nowakowska recalls attendees at the Library Association Book Fair giving the Darth Vader cut-out wide berth as they moved down the aisle. While the media focused heavily on Grand Moff Tarkin, being portrayed by well-known horror film regular Peter Cushing, the fans had latched onto his villainous counterpart. The mask symbolized the villain's separation from humanity and his supernatural powers, a popular horror movie device with mythological roots going back to the masks of the pharaohs. Yet the suit and helmet recalled the nobility of knights and samurai, bound to codes of honor. The idea of Vader, who he was and where he fit into the storytelling framework, was circling around in fans' minds and elevated him to cult status before anyone had seen the film.

Star Wars burst onto the silver screen as an amalgamation of genres. It reflected the adventures of Flash Gordon space operas, the gritty reality of Westerns, and the nobility of Arthurian legends. Sometimes forgotten is George Lucas's clue to the principal intended audience—children—by opening the movie with the fairy tale inspired words, "A long time ago, in a galaxy far, far away...." Folklore passed down orally from generation to generation became written down in fables and fairy tales. In those legends, the villains were the obstacle to the happy ending. They represented the embodiment of evil that children can't quite comprehend but know exists, like Obi-Wan's missing planet in *Attack of the Clones*.

At first blush, Darth Vader's role in 1977 seemed little more than the fairy tale's necessary bogeyman, an implacable dark enforcer for the evil Empire. Even from the beginning, though, hints of the character's true depth peek through. Princess Leia boldly talks back to him and Grand Moff Tarkin has superior authority to him, while even a few simple lines of dialogue reveal that the hermit Ben Kenobi, an exiled Jedi Knight, has a long and tragic backstory with the murderous Vader. *The Complete Vader* quotes 1977 fanzine issues calling Vader, "a shining exemplar of chivalry" and "probably the most popular character in *Star Wars*," and Windham notes that, "most tellingly, the early fanzines cast him as the tragic figure in countless fan-generated stories, demonstrating a desire to elevate Vader to mythic status." Though the Vader onscreen in the first film has no real character journey, his portrayal— a rare combination of imposing physicality from David Prowse and masterfully measured voice-acting by James Earl Jones— inspired fans to imagine the possibilities of how a good man could become a monster.

VADER'S BEST MOMENTS ARE THE ONES THAT REVEAL THAT HE IS NOT SIMPLY RAGE-FILLED AND INDISCRIMINATELY EVIL.

MACHINE TO MAN

In *The Empire Strikes Back* and *Return of the Jedi*, Lucas delivered on the promise of Vader's potential as a villain with character depth. Vader's best moments are the ones that reveal he is not simply rage-filled and indiscriminately evil, but a man of complex motivations and goals. The brutal Sith Lord is still there, asphyxiating an admiral for his incompetence, altering the deal with Lando, and arriving to personally ensure timely completion of the second Death Star by whatever means necessary. Yet the helmet comes off—first seen only in a glimpse from behind, to preserve the mystery—to confirm the character's underlying humanity. When Vader tells Luke that, "I am your father," the biggest point for speculation in 1980 wasn't the revelation, but whether the Dark Lord was telling the truth or a manipulative lie. Ultimately, Luke's willingness to die a good man rather than fall to the dark side inspires Vader to find the courage and strength to make the right choice. His final act is to insist upon seeing Luke, "with my own eyes," at last returning to the man he always had been capable of being. Vader's is not a hero's journey, but a tragedy of a life surrendered to evil. Only at the end does he find redemption in an ultimate act of self-sacrifice, finally rediscovering his true self.

This page, from left:
Luke fights for the soul
of his father; Vader
faces Obi-Wan Kenobi
again in their final
duel; the imposing
Lord Vader.

Opposite page,
clockwise from left:
A crucial moment in the
final battle between
Luke and his father; the
subservient Sith Lord;
Vader faces Luke in
a battle that takes
unexpected twists.

ANAKIN IS VADER

In hindsight it may be easy to forget that many *Star Wars* fans experienced a shocking revelation in 2005 just as powerful as the one felt in 1980. When Darth Vader leads legions of troopers to attack the Jedi Temple and slaughter everyone inside, he is not the iconic Dark Lord in the mask—he is youthful and vital, not yet mutilated by a terrible duel amid lava, still Anakin Skywalker in everything but his intentions. With this simple and stunning visual, George Lucas makes a truly powerful thematic point: Darth Vader is Anakin Skywalker, and Anakin is Vader. They are not two characters, but one.

By its nature, the prequel trilogy portrayed a three-movie character arc for Anakin, in which he undertakes the initial stages of a hero's journey before his fateful choices propel his life and the galaxy into tragedy. *The Phantom Menace* establishes the roots of his later decisions in the circumstances of Anakin's childhood as a slave. Most importantly, his mother, Shmi, shows him that sometimes we must let go of others out of love, but the Jedi fails to nurture that lesson. *Attack of the Clones* more fully fleshes out Anakin's path as a metaphor for the fall of the Jedi Order, as Palpatine's manipulations begin to isolate Anakin from the Jedi while galactic war begins to separate the Order from their roles as peacekeepers and followers of the Force. As *Revenge of the Sith* draws to a close, Anakin loses not just his limbs but also his mentor Obi-Wan, his wife, Padmé, and his confidant Palpatine, now his Master. He once more becomes a slave, but this time to his own fears.

More recently, *The Clone Wars* added depth to Anakin and how his tragic arc parallels the fall of the Jedi Order that believed him to be the Chosen One. While the Jedi as individuals had become powerful protectors, the insidious toll of war and loss distracted them from their most important calling, to be compassionate counselors of the beings they were honor-bound to serve. Just as Obi-Wan cleaved Anakin's limbs from his body, so, too, had Darth Sidious meticulously sliced away vital pieces of the Republic's Jedi Order until it was rendered impotent.

ANAKIN HIDES BEHIND THE MASK OF DARTH VADER, LITERALLY AND FIGURATIVELY.

A REFLECTION OF WHO WE ARE

I didn't always connect with Anakin, but I met many fellow fans over the years who wrote or spoke eloquently about him. One woman seemed to have a particularly keen empathy for Darth Vader, and I asked her about what inspired her affinity for him. She explained how she saw her son—a good young man who had made a bad choice and was then forced to live with it—in Vader. As she related her own personal experience, the relevance of Darth Vader as a hero-turned-villain began to resonate with me. While the character draws on various elements of myth, the familiarity of human nature is also embedded in his story. Even if the stakes are not so high, the tragedies not so great, everyone can relate to the journey Vader travels as a character. Each of us makes choices we regret, and we must bear the consequences, sometimes for years.

Beyond the simple admission of his starting point for his *Star Wars* hero and villain, George Lucas' legacy as a whole reveals that storytellers not only draw upon their own selves in creating characters, but also the reality of the era in which they live. Reminders of world-stage conflict are peppered throughout the saga, from the Nazi-like Imperials and nail-biting dogfights in space that harken back to World War II, to the callous disregard for clones' lives by the Republic they defended and the morally complicated, unwinnable Clone Wars reminiscent of the Vietnam War. Anakin represents the good men and women called upon to be heroes, to serve on the front line, and he provides a stark reminder of the costs of war to their bodies and their psyches beyond the battlefield.

With his friends and family dead and the galaxy conquered, Vader can no longer find a reason to continue to accept his own humanity. He cannot cope with being Anakin, the man who made terrible choices, so he hides behind the mask of Darth Vader, literally and figuratively. Only decades later does Luke break through the façade, giving Vader a reason to rediscover the Anakin who never stopped existing. This hopelessness of a lost soul resonates with us in the real world, too. People can become stuck in vicious cycles of addiction, mental illness, post-traumatic stress disorder, abusive relationships, and others. Sometimes all they need to find a way out is for someone to reach out a hand, to connect with them on a human level, as Luke does with Darth Vader. Though the tragedy of Anakin Skywalker is a cautionary tale, his redemption can be an inspiration for all of us to rise above the choices we regret. ✪

BEING BISECTED BY A JEDI AND
PLUNGING DOWN A SEEMINGLY
BOTTOMLESS PIT WOULD
ORDINARILY PROVE FATAL—
BUT NOT FOR DARTH MAUL!
SAM WITWER PLAYS THE
LONG LOST WARRIOR
IN *STAR WARS: THE
CLONE WARS'*
EPIC SEASON
CONCLUSION.

BACK FROM THE
DEPTHS!

Star Wars Insider: Before you were cast, what was your opinion of Darth Maul?

Sam Witwer: The thing with Darth Maul is that we all want to know more about him. He shows up and creates this incredible impression—and then he's gone! We've all been clamoring for him to return. The fun thing about these episodes of *Star Wars: The Clone Wars* is that we learn a little bit about what he's been doing for the last 10 years and it's not good. He's been uncomfortable.

What did you think when you found out Darth Maul was returning, and that you would be playing the role?

Dave Filoni [executive editor] hinted that he might have something for me after the Mortis episodes [in which Witwer voiced the role of the Son—Ed], and so I was naturally curious. I assumed it was going to be some bounty hunter or something, which I would have been thrilled with. When he informed me that they needed an actor to play Darth Maul,

I just had a geek-stroke and lost the power of speech! Dave not only said that he wanted me to play Darth Maul, but that he wanted to take it in sort of a "Gollum" direction. When I read the script I saw what he meant, but also saw that this might be an opportunity to take it in a "Colonel Kurtz" [from *Apocolyse Now*] direction.

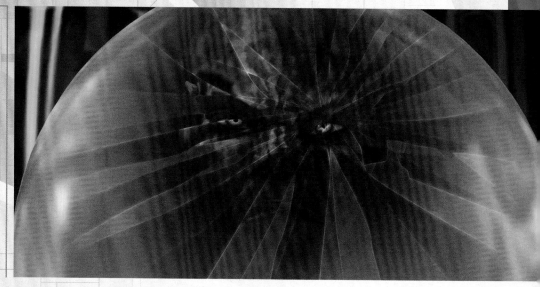

Right: Darth Maul's hotly anticipated return to the *Star Wars* universe was first hinted at in the haunting coda to season three's "Witches of the Mist."

Far right: Savage Opress is reunited with his long lost brother. Will they be able to get revenge on the Jedi?

How did this influence the character?
We decided that he might be pitiful one moment and dangerous the next, creating this maelstrom of conflicting emotions and unpleasantness. We all have our opinions about who he is, and that creates expectations, so what do we do? We blow away all expectations and say he's insane! It makes perfect sense. If you're going to be dispatched in the way he was, there must be huge consequences for having him come back. He can't just come back with mechanical legs and say, "I'm the same old Darth Maul that I ever was." There was a major cost, and it's consistent with the other things we see in the movies.

Palpatine says that the dark side of the Force leads to abilities that some would consider to be unnatural, and one of those things is cheating death. The Sith see death as defeat. The Jedi see it as the natural progression of things. The Sith don't look at it that way; they want to control everything. You can't gain any more power if you die, so one of the things that all the Sith do is try to preserve themselves at all cost.

For example Darth Vader is all about that. He gets burned and put in a suit, but that's somehow preferable to death. In a way, Darth Maul has done something similar. He's wallowed in these caves, eating garbage, living in these horrible conditions. Through all his grief and connection with the dark side of the Force, these spider legs made of garbage have grown out of him as manifestations of his pain.

> "HE CAN'T JUST COME BACK WITH MECHANICAL LEGS AND SAY, 'I'M THE SAME OLD DARTH MAUL THAT I EVER WAS.'"

How do you feel about the character now that you've played him?
He's a fearful man. He feels that his rage and hatred have kept him alive, along with his fear of death. He has a twisted sense of humor and he's far more dangerous than people realize. I looked at him as purely muscle: He was the ultimate hitman. But we learn that he's also potentially a general. He's tactically minded, strategically minded, very smart and politically savvy. He was raised by Palpatine— or so we've understood—so he's good at things that you might not expect.

Let's also not forget that Darth Maul perhaps was intended to participate in the Clone Wars. Maybe he was supposed to be General Grievous or even Count Dooku? There was a plan for him, a purpose for him and all of that was stripped away by Obi-Wan.

BROTHERLY LOVE?

Sam Witwer: "It's sad to see how hard Darth Maul works just to get back at Obi-Wan; it's kind of tragic, especially when you take into account Savage and where he sits with all this. Savage is not necessarily a bad guy, or at least didn't start out that way. We can imply from Savage's back-story that Maul had a similar story. We explore that a little bit, too. I think the relationship between Maul and Savage is very interesting as Maul will eventually look upon Savage as his apprentice."

FIRST IMPRESSIONS

Sam Witwer: "I went to a sneak preview of Episode I the day before it opened. After the movie, we noticed that there was a line at a nearby theater for some guy named Ray Park. So we went and met Ray Park. He was a total sweetheart to us and this was just before the film was going to open that night, out there in Skokie, Illinois!

"My first impression of Darth Maul was at once, this brutal, dangerous, terrifying warrior and Ray Park who was just the nicest, coolest guy you could ever meet. I think between those two experiences—seeing the movie and meeting Ray—that this character really has a special place in my heart.

"The next time I met Ray was years later. I wasn't even an actor when I saw first saw Episode I. I met Ray and I tried to explain to him, 'You know, Ray, this is gonna sound weird, but in a videogame, I sort of fight you!' I tried to explain the whole Force Unleashed connection, but I don't know if he understood what I was saying because I was geeking out! Then a week later, we were both signing at a convention and I'm like, 'OK, you see now? I'm sort of a Star Wars character, too! He's a wonderful guy."

How has he changed?
In the first two episodes, we focus on the madness of what's happened to him, how he's been disabled for a decade, and lost a lot of what he was trained as. The way he speaks is muddled and he's not the same person he once was.

In the next episode—after he is reunited with Savage and gets put back together a little bit—he still doesn't quite know where his place is, but we do get that ultimate dark warrior that we were hoping to see back. We see pretty much exactly what we thought we were going to see: a very angry, very efficient warrior who wants nothing more than to fight Obi-Wan Kenobi.

As the story continues, he realizes that fighting and destroying Obi-Wan ultimately isn't satisfying. He has many opportunities to kill Obi-Wan, but he keeps prolonging it and realizes that this has to last; he's been dreaming about it for 10 years and can't just kill Obi-Wan quickly! He starts developing plans and aspirations, but at the center of those aspirations is, ultimately, revenge against Kenobi.

What was it like to record these episodes with Clancy Brown (Savage Opress) and James Arnold Taylor (Obi-Wan)?
I love the way James plays Obi-Wan! No matter how much you beat that guy up, he'll always have some snarky response; he's like Indiana Jones!

I've been a big fan of Clancy since I was a kid, going back to *Highlander* and *The Shawshank Redemption*. I met him when I was doing the Mortis trilogy last season. He brought his son in because he wanted autographs from the people that were working on *The Clone Wars*, and I had no idea that Clancy was part of the show. I was recording the Mortis episodes and Clancy walks in and says, "Hey, you're the apprentice from The Force Unleashed, will you sign an autograph for my kid?" It was weird—he should have been signing autographs for *me* not the other way around!

"MAUL STARTS DEVELOPING PLANS AND ASPIRATIONS, BUT AT THE CENTER OF THOSE ASPIRATIONS IS REVENGE AGAINST KENOBI!"

Dave Filoni was talking about some sort of story point and how it would relate to The Force Unleashed and Clancy starts piping in about "Well, in The Force Unleashed, this happened..." He really knows his stuff! He's a tremendously well-respected actor and here he is talking to Dave about "my" videogame!

When we were recording, I was so nervous. I think I've settled into it now, but in that first session I felt like the pressure was on. Dave and Clancy were cracking jokes, and I think someone mentioned to me about loosening up and I said, "If I mess this up, millions of fans are going to be mad at me!" Dave Filoni's like, "Welcome to my world, pal. Now read the lines!"

AN AMERICAN SITH?

Sam Witwer: "I know that Darth Maul has an English accent in *The Phantom Menace*, but we didn't worry about that because he's been eating garbage for 10 years and that's going to slightly change the way you talk! But don't worry. We made sure there were moments when he sounds like his old self."

REUNITED WITH VADER AND FRIENDS!

"I had a lot of *Star Wars* toys when I was a kid, but alas, they were either given away or thrown away—or so I thought! My mother recently found my Darth Vader Collector's Case with tons of my old figures. I was stunned. I really thought all that stuff was gone."

Top of this page: Sam Witwer records a scene as the evil Darth Maul for *The Clone Wars*.

Left: Ready for revenge? Darth Maul plots the downfall of Obi-Wan Kenobi.

Right: Can Obi-Wan survive another encounter with his nemesis?

"WHEN WE WERE DEVELOPING STARKILLER, WE THOUGHT OF HIM AS AN INTERPRETATION OF DARTH MAUL, IN PART."

RED MENACE!

George Lucas described Darth Maul as "a figure from your worst nightmare," leading designer Iain McCaig to offer Lucas a design based on a nightmare of his, which although rejected, would later inspire the Nightsisters from *Star Wars: The Clone Wars*.

McCaig's eventual illustration used his own face adorned with markings blending a "flayed flesh face," face-painting of African tribes and Rorschach experimentation [spilling ink onto paper, folding it in half and opening it to produce a pattern—Ed]

Darth Maul's head originally had feathers, which were interpreted by the design team as horns.

THE FUTURE...

Sam Witwer: "Darth Maul will be around for a while in the show. The story takes some really interesting turns, but the psychology of the character is very, very well thought out. It's deep stuff! He's not just a mustache-twirling villain; there's a lot more going on there—there's pain and there's suffering. I don't know how the audience is going to react, but I actually feel sorry for the guy. It'll be interesting if the audience does as well by the time we're done."

You've embodied the dark side before, as the Emperor, Starkiller, and the Son. How is each role different for you?

Those roles are extraordinarily different. When we were developing the character of Starkiller, we thought of him as an interpretation of Darth Maul in part. We created this little geek formula where Starkiller was two parts Han Solo, one part Luke Skywalker, one part Indiana Jones, and one part Darth Maul. Any time that Starkiller was talking to Darth Vader, Darth Maul became the inspiration— I thought he should behave more like Darth Maul did in the film. When Starkiller addresses Lord Vader, he sort of assumes that Sith-like posture and voice. Palpatine has the manipulative edge and a wonderful sense of humor, at least when things are going his way.

Since he'd been trained by Palpatine as his protégé, he would've taken a lot from that guy. So we borrowed heavily from Palpatine for Darth Maul and I think he's a much more dangerous character when you realize how smart he is.

The Son was an arrogant character. I felt Darth Maul had to be extremely arrogant; that starts causing trouble for him later, but you don't necessarily see that at first. It's cool because there's a little bit of connection to the Mortis episodes that the fans will pick up on.

I read a scene in the script where Darth Maul is ranting and raving. I was doing my research, and as soon as I read that Darth Maul was muttering to himself, I found myself wondering, "Well what is he muttering about? What has he told himself in order to keep himself alive?" Part of it is remembering his training, so I started bringing pieces of the Sith Code into the mutterings. There is a thought that the Sith had this code that's a mockery of the Jedi Code. It's things like "Peace is a lie" and "There is only power in strength" and all this great stuff. As I was reading that there was this moment where it said something about "Through victory my chains are broken." Immediately I thought, *Yeah, the chains...*

When I was recording the speech that the Son delivers to Ahsoka before he turns her to the dark side —"The chains are the easy part; it's what goes on in here that's hard"—I was ad-libbing and threw that line in. I love how they feature it; there's this moment when Maul is getting disjointed bits of the Sith Code out, trying to remember his training and then he gets to this point where he recites this line about the chains. It makes his insanity specific in that way.

There are things that he talks about that you'll have to turn up the audio and listen to very carefully. ☸

Left: Starkiller from The Force Unleashed and The Force Unleashed II and The Son from Season Three's intriguing "Mortis" story arc.

Below: Witwer in full flow as he delivers a speech as Darth Maul.

WITWER'S WORLD

Sam Witwer was born in 1977, making him the same age as the *Star Wars* saga! He has appeared in individual episodes of numerous television shows as well as playing minor recurring characters in shows such as *Battlestar Galactica*, *Smallville*, *CSI: Crime Scene Investigation*, and *Dexter*. He also played the main protagonist, Galen Marek/Starkiller, in the *Star Wars: The Force Unleashed* videogame and its sequel. He can currently be seen in the US/Canadian remake of the BBC's supernatural drama series *Being Human*.

On the big screen, he has appeared in *Crank*, *The Mist*, and *Gamer*.

His talents also extend to music, and he fronts his own band: The Crashtones! Check them out at www.samwitwer.com

Speak like a Sith

SITH LANGUAGE CREATOR BEN GROSSBLATT OFFERS A CRASH COURSE ON THE FINER POINTS OF THE MOST EVIL LANGUAGE IN THE GALAXY!

In November, 2010, I was given an assignment right up my alley: Invent a Sith language for *Book of Sith*, a collection of Sith history, philosophy, and artifacts (available from Amazon).

My goal in developing Sith was to create a plausible, linguistically sound language. Plausible, in that it would sound and feel real—not like a cartoonish language for the bad guys to speak. (I wouldn't be putting sentences like *Glotch blug bodge!* in the mouths of the Sith.) Linguistically sound, in that it would conform to patterns and principles of (human) language. This is the way to achieve a language with the depth and richness that the *Star Wars* galaxy demands.

I faced more practical considerations, too. For instance, Sith had to look pronounceable. Otherwise, no one would

even bother trying to speak it. The words would just lie there on the page. I knew that Sith would have no "words" like *r'rhhoqtk*.

The first step was settling on what linguists call a segment inventory—a list of the phonemes (speech sounds) employed by a language. Combined with a system of phonotactics (the ways phonemes are put together), this would give the Sith language its personality, its unique feel. In order for the language to come alive and embody fans' ideas of the Sith, the language would need to be realistic, of course, but it would also need to *sound right*.

Sith needed to feel martial and mystical. You had to be able to imagine it carved into temple façades, painted on tattered banners, and yelled from parapets. It needed to work as a suitable, aesthetically-pleasing vehicle for

communication among the feared and misunderstood Sith—for curses, chants, conspiracies. To that end, I imagined a tough—but not barbarous—language, one that could convey a kind of confident, elegant cruelty. And Sith would have to ring with authority so you could envision it functioning among elites of the dark side the way Latin functioned in Europe for centuries: as a repository of culture and learning.

To achieve a formal, quasi-military quality, I preferred the frequent use of closed syllables (syllables ending with consonants) to make brisk, choppy words.

chwûq — "ember"

hâsk — "anguish"

ajak — "doctrine"

A note for language nerds

In rendering Sith words in the Roman alphabet, I use two special symbols: [û] stands for the vowel sound in *club*. [â] stands for the vowel sound in *bash*. Those symbols aren't part of the IPA (International Phonetic Alphabet), but I wanted to avoid symbols that "civilians" would find completely unfamiliar.

Giving Sith a mystical feel was more of an art than a science. I hoped to evoke a kind of ancient strangeness with consonant clusters like nw-, dzw-, and tsy-.

nwûl	"peace"
dzwol	"to exist, abide"
tsyoq	"to squeeze with the hand"

Translation headaches

Because of its limited phonetic palette, creating Sith versions of *Star Wars* names can be tricky. Take the name *Palpatine*. Sith doesn't have a "p" sound, and no Sith words have an "ee" sound in a closed syllable or an *l* between consonants. The closest a Sith speaker with a heavy accent could come to replicating the Emperor's name might be *Marmûtin* (or "mar-muh-tin"). I like to think creative Sith scribes would translate His Excellency's name into their own language. If the basis of his name was the same as the word *palpitare* ("to throb"), then the Sith equivalent of his name might be *Chirikyât* ("chee-ree-kyatt"), or "He Who Causes Them to Throb and Tremble in Fear."

Given that Sith might have appeared on pedestals and pillars, and in the dark declarations of tyrants, I wanted the words themselves to be like monuments. Imposing, undeniable. Words like steles recording the names of sinister heroes. To my mind, long, intricate words suggested something about the language's structure; Sith would be an agglutinative language. That is, a language, like Turkish, that builds words by stringing together many meaningful parts.

The Knotters of Entrails (alchemists who created Sithspawn, as described in *Book of Sith*) would be known in Sith as *Ninûshwodzakut*. That jawbreaker is built from four separate chunks, like so:

nin	+ûsh	+ wodza	+ kut
"tie, knot"	agentive marker	"intestines"	collective plural marker

The phrase "because of dreaming about a demon" is rendered in Sith as a single, towering word—*kûskutsiqsayanjat*:

kûsk	+ ut	+ siqsa	+ anjat
"to dream"	nominal marker (of verbs)	"demon"	ablative marker

Accent these lexical Goliaths on the first syllable—every Sith word is stressed that way—and they take on a looming, teetering quality, as if they might collapse and crush you.

Sith Scribing

Beyond these and other abstract concepts that appealed to the linguistics wonk in me, there was also a writing system to invent. I wanted this version of Sith writing to lend itself to calligraphy—the *Book of Sith* Holocron contained a scrap of Sith burial shroud, after all—as well as to printing and inscribing (imagine 10-foot-high Sith letters chiseled into stone slabs).

The Sith alphabet (the Kittât):

t	i "heat" "hit"		tw
d			dw
k	â "hat"		mw
q		tw	nw
m	u "suit" "soot"	dw	tsw
n		mw	dzw
ts	û "hut"	nw	ty
dz		tsw	dy
s	o "toad"	dzw	my
z			ny
h	a "ah"	ty	tsy
ch		dy	dzy
j	oi "toy"	my	
sh		ny	
r/l	ai "buy"	tsy	
w		dzy	
y			

Note that some consonants combine with w and y to form complex characters:

Putting it all together—the phonology, the morphology, the syntax, and the writing system—means we can produce things like this, the Sith version of the Rule of Two:

The Rule of Two
Chwayatyun
chwayat + yun
"rule, law" + "two"

Two there should be;
Dzworokka yun
dzwol + okka yun
"to exist, abide" + hortatory "two"
mood

no more, no less.
nyâshqûwai, nwiqûwai

nyâsh	+ qû	+ wai	nwi	+ qû	+ wai
"big, much, many"	+ comparative	+ negation	"small, few"	+ comparative	+ negation

One to embody power,
Wotok tsawakmidwanottoi.

wo	+ tok	tsawak	+ midwan	+ ottoi
"one"	+ ordinal number marker	"embodiment"	"power"	dative marker

the other to crave it.
Yuntok hyarutmidwanottoi.

yun	+ tok	hyal	+ ut	+ midwan	+ ottoi
"two"	ordinal number marker	"to crave"	nominal marker (of verbs)	"power"	dative marker

There's more to say about Sith (and *in* Sith), but these basics are enough to express the mood and character of the language of the dark side.

Qorit ("The End")

Ben Grossblatt is a senior editor at becker&mayer!, the bookmakers who developed and produced *Book of Sith* and its Holocron case as well as *The Jedi Path*. Ben discovered *Star Wars* in 1977 and earned a Master's degree in linguistics in '97. His last name translated into Sith is Dzunyâsh.

WHY THE *STAR WARS*
SAGA'S SEQUEL BAD
GUY IS DANGEROUS.
WORDS: BRYAN YOUNG

"Villains have been so important in film history," Roger Ebert once said, "you could almost argue there wouldn't be movies without them. Film is the most dynamic storytelling known to man and it lends itself to melodrama and conflict: good guys versus bad guys." And of *Star Wars* specifically, he said that, "each film is only as good as its villain."

It's hard to argue with a man held as the gold standard of film criticism, and it's through this lens we'll be taking a look at Kylo Ren and what he adds to *Star Wars: The Force Awakens*.

Through the entire classic saga, the heroes of the Republic, then the Rebellion, are plagued by the phantom menace, Darth Sidious, and his grand plan for the Sith. Along the way he had some of the most fearsome right hands of doom, from Darth Maul and Count Dooku to General Grievous before finally settling on the worst of them all: Darth Vader. Each of these villains were some of the best

THE POWER OF THE DARK SIDE: KYLO REN

to grace the silver screen, but the shadow of Darth Vader looms large in the newest installment of the Skywalker saga of *Star Wars* films.

We talked to a number of *Star Wars* experts about what they think makes a great villain and how Kylo Ren stacks up to this standard.

Paul S. Kemp is the author of *Lords of the Sith*, which made him a logical first choice to turn to:

"A great villain is one whose villainy makes sense, whose drives are understandable, even if not sympathetic. We don't know all of Kylo's backstory, but he appears in some ways to have been a failure, as both an aspiring Jedi and perhaps also as a son. That sense of failure and the insecurity it creates festered, and to overcome both he turned to Vader, who—to Kylo—embodied strength, confidence, power, and maybe even served as a kind of proxy father figure since Han, obviously, did not. That's all relatable, right? We can understand that. Of course, emulating Vader doesn't actually fill his emotional holes, so he piles frustration and rage onto his insecurity and *boom*, we've got this emotionally rich character who vacillates between a rage-filled teenager and a frightening would-be Sith Lord. He's a character on the edge—or the bridge, if you prefer—and we're watching his formative years.

I found even the small glimpse of him we got in the film to be a fascinating one."

Holly Frey is the host of the top-rated podcast *Stuff You Missed in History Class*, but is also an intense *Star Wars* fan who writes for *StarWars.com*:

"To me, the ingredients for making a great villain are: intensity, style, charisma, unpredictability, and a steadfast belief that their cause is just.

In Kylo Ren, we're seeing the kernel of a true villain—almost like a villain embryo. He's got all the ingredients, and we're actually getting to see the evil soufflé bake. That makes for an interesting ride, because you don't actually know how it will turn out. Seeing a villain wobble in their development is really compelling.

On a scale of Ozzel to Greedo, both great villains that I love, I'd wager Kylo Ren is somewhere around Bossk, which is high praise indeed."

C. Robert Cargill is a long time film critic, the author of *Dreams and Shadows,* and is the screenwriter of upcoming *Dr. Strange* motion picture for Marvel Studios. Here's his take on Kylo Ren:

"A great villain has to be more than just an obstacle; they have to mean something to the audience, to the story. They have to represent some ideal or philosophy or concept that makes them more than just something we want to see stopped. They have to deepen the story every bit as much as the hero does. The most interesting thing about Kylo Ren is the meta nature of him. Here we have a movie that wants to live up to the legend of a nearly 40-year-old franchise, and in it

> "A GREAT VILLAIN HAS TO BE MORE THAN JUST AN OBSTACLE; THEY HAVE TO MEAN SOMETHING TO THE AUDIENCE, TO THE STORY."
> —C. ROBERT CARGILL

we have a villain that wants to live up to the legend of the villain in that franchise. Ren is always grasping for that legend, trying to live up to it, worried at every moment that he might not be able to be the man his grandfather was—that he might fail himself, his grandfather, and in a very meta way, us, the audience. It's a bold thematic statement worn on its sleeve and I admire it for that."

is a legendary name amongst *Star Wars* fans, as he wrote *I, Jedi*, and the first five books of the X-Wing series, among others.

"A good villain is driven, internally consistent, ruthless and remorseless and, for me, elegant. Kylo Ren hits most of those attributes pretty well. I the presentation and I am looking forward to seeing what happens next."

Amy Ratcliffe is a world-renowned expert on *Star Wars*, a fellow contributor to *Star Wars Insider*, and co-host of the *Full of Sith* podcast:

"The most interesting villains are conflicted ones. I want someone who is unsure and pulled between good and bad, light and dark. I'm also fascinated by villains who act based on righteous intentions. That's incredibly dangerous. And Kylo Ren—he is unquestionably torn. He wants to be as cold and ruthless as Darth Vader, but he feels a pull to the light. His emotions, rash behavior, and uncertainty make him fascinating.

Kylo Ren is the villain *Star Wars* needed. In some ways, he's a parallel of Luke. When Luke underwent his training, he was focused on pursuing the light side but he was tempted, albeit briefly, by the dark side. Kylo's dealing

> **"KYLO REN IS THE VILLAIN *STAR WARS* NEEDED. IN SOME WAYS, HE'S A PARALLEL OF LUKE." —AMY RATCLIFFE**

with the opposite, and it makes him a formidable threat, and more nuanced than the villains who have come before him. In the scene when Kylo kills his father, I tear up first when Kylo says, 'I'm being torn apart.' His emotion is so raw. I've never felt that from another villain in *Star Wars*."

As the author of *Aftermath*, the first book bridging the divide between *Return of the Jedi* and *The Force Awakens*, Chuck Wendig wouldn't let us *not* take his opinion on Kylo Ren's villainy:

"For me, a villain at the surface has to be cool and has to be scary, right? Like, you need someone who is a real bad news kind of character, someone who enters the scene and, with presence, lets you feel awe in the truest sense of the word. But that's not really enough, to me. You have to go deeper, you have to have a villain who has more going on—remember, villains don't know they're the villains. They think they're the heroes! They are the protagonists of their own story. Vader is great when he first steps onto the *Tantive IV*, but he gets

really interesting with *The Empire Strikes Back* when you learn that he's—uh, spoiler—Luke's father. That utterly complicates both his and Luke's mission and lends an emotional challenge that wasn't there before. Kylo Ren gets that complication earlier, right out of the gate with *The Force Awakens*—he's far more human than Vader is, and far earlier in his journey of transformation to the dark side, too. He's scary because he's familiar to us. He's scary because he's human—not some killing machine, but a person who believes—or who is gaslighting himself into believing—in the crusade he's undertaking. For me, a great villain is the sort that can have a conversation with the hero, because you know it's going to be a *fascinating* conversation. When I look for examples of great

villains, one that I always come to is René Belloq from *Raiders of the Lost Ark*, every conversation he has with Indiana Jones reminds the audience that he's merely a shadowy reflection of our hero. Kylo Ren does the same for Han Solo, not only in their one scene together, but through every other interaction he has as well. We see that all of the elements that made Han Solo and Anakin Skywalker great characters separately combine to make a monster.

Kylo Ren is every bit the shadow of Luke as he is his own father and grandfather. Where Luke would rather kill himself than kill or join his father in the dark side, Kylo Ren would rather kill his father than embrace the light.

It's a stunning parallel that allows us to add Kylo Ren to the pantheon of *Star Wars* villains and we know that he will hold his own amongst that number."

ADAM DRIVER IS
KYLO REN

THE MYSTERIOUS KYLO REN, AS PLAYED BY ADAM DRIVER, MENACES OUR HEROES IN *STAR WARS: THE FORCE AWAKENS*

Clockwise, from above: Kylo Ren stalks our heroes; the imposing and mysterious Kylo Ren; taking command of the First Order troops on Jakku.

Star Wars Insider: How did you get involved with *The Force Awakens*?

Adam Driver: I think it was the last day of shooting *Girls* and I got a phone call to see if I was interested in meeting J.J. Abrams to talk about *Star Wars*. I thought that it would be interesting to do, so I said "yes." A month later, I left for LA and I met J.J. to talk about the role. Then I met with Kathleen Kennedy, who talked more about it. I was very excited. It's such a big thing and I've never done anything quite like this with this many

something that he talked about the most. I feel like some of the movies are so heavy on special effects or visuals and lot of things get lost as far as two people talking to one another. And that was something that J.J. stressed from the beginning; It was all character—there was hardly any talk of special effects. When we originally met and talked, it was all about grounding these people in a reality, even though it's a long time ago in a galaxy far, far away. If no one cares about what's happening or no one believes that these people are real, then you won't care about any of it.

"THERE'S SOMETHING EMPOWERING FOR SOMEONE TO COMPLETELY HIDE THEMSELVES IN A MASK THAT IS SO INTIMIDATING."

moving pieces. Wearing a mask is quite a challenging thing. It was very scary and terrifying, so it wasn't something that immediately seemed like a "yes." Actually, I thought about it quite a bit, even though it was kind of a no-brainer, but I didn't want to take it lightly.

How much was J.J. Abrams able to share with you after you signed on?
J.J. Abrams pretty much walked me through the whole thing. He talked about how he wanted to start it and the themes that he was going with. He talked about things that inspired him that he and Lawrence Kasdan were already working on. There have been small changes since then, but it's all pretty much the same. J.J. had ideas that were very clear in his mind about the conventions that he wanted to upturn and things that grounded Kylo Ren as a character. Character was

What sense did you have of taking on such a role?
The idea of doing it is a scary thing. Even though J.J. mapped out what that character does, he left out a lot of things for us to discover. He wanted to get my input, which was a huge thing also in a movie of this scale. Suddenly you have a director who wants you to be involved in making it, and given the history of these movies, that's very exciting. I was a fan of the *Star Wars* movies when I was younger, so suddenly to work on it in my adult life and have input seems unbelievable.

Did you enjoy working on practical sets?
Everything is so real. I think grounding everything in a reality is more effective. Not to get on a high horse about technology, but sometimes it's in place of something that's real and tactile and I think that people take it for granted.

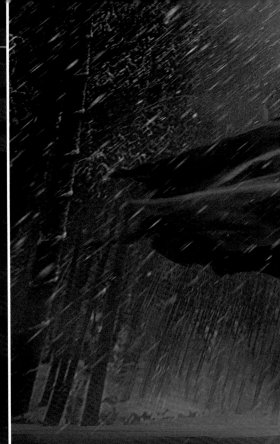

I've actually read the *Making of Star Wars*, and learning how all those people were doing things out of this need to do something different. The conventional way of making a movie at that time and special effects were very important, but it was all about people collaborating in a room together trying to figure out a way to make it real.

As an actor, is it freeing or limiting to wear the mask?
It's both. I get here for three or four days to shoot, and I put all this stuff on, the mask and the costume, then I put it away for a few weeks. Then I come back to it. It was such an evolving thing up until the days we started working on it. Then you're thrown into it, and boom! Then suddenly I can't see the ground. They are all good challenges. As we've been shooting, I find it more freeing. The physical life is really important. There are so many layers to him anyway. It's interesting to find out who he is with the mask on or with the mask off, and that was part of our initial conversations. There's something empowering for someone to completely hide themselves in a mask that is so intimidating.

Did you talk to J.J. Abrams and costume designer Michael Kaplan about the look of Kylo Ren at all?

Clockwise, from above: Early concept art showing Kylo Ren's helmet in detail; more concept art showing Kylo Ren in a rare, reflective mood; poised for action; Adam Driver on set, shooting the razing of Jakku.

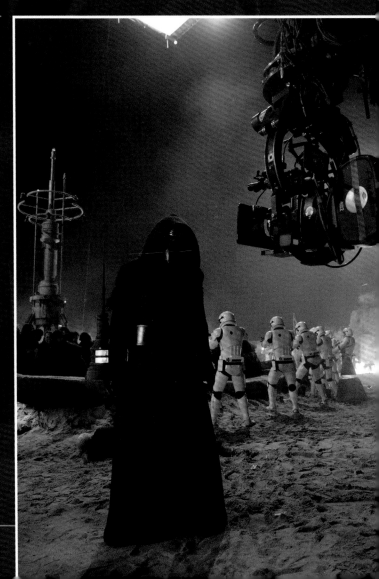

Was the table read a surreal experience?
Seeing everybody all in one room for the table read was surreal; I just wanted to sit back as an audience member and listen to them. I remember in the read-through that things would just come to life when the original characters read their parts. Suddenly I just wanted to sit back and watch and enjoy the movie, but then I realized I had lines to say and a part to play. I got to act across from people who have no idea that they are very much a part of my youth.

What makes *Star Wars* great?
At the end of it, I think the great thing about *Star Wars* is that, yes, it's a long time ago in a galaxy far, far away and there are spaceships and lightsabers, but the family story and the friendship and sacrifice elements are really big, human themes that make it enduring. All those human things are what connected people to those movies in the first place. It's never been taken lightly, and there's always been a conversation that starts with putting the humanity in it.

"I'D FLY IN TO SEE WHAT THEY WERE COMING UP WITH AND SEE NODS TO AKIRA KUROSAWA, AND HIS JACKET THAT BOWS OUT A BIT, LIKE A SAMURAI."

It was such an evolving thing. I'd fly in to see what they were coming up with and see nods to Akira Kurosawa, and his jacket that bows out just a little bit, like a samurai, and all those references. Then I'd leave for two weeks and come back to see how it was shaped a little more. My only input was whether it felt good or bad. I was involved in making it functional, which was great. They were all about how they could make it more efficient and something that someone could wear. It looks great, but if you can't move in it or breathe in it, then it doesn't make sense for the audience or the actor.

How did you go about conveying the character's physicality?
Trying to convey someone whose physical life is very much about combat and fighting in a short amount of time is a challenging thing. One of the first things I wanted to do, as soon as everything was all scheduled, was to start drilling daily and making it part of my daily life. I had three months

to prepare, so I wanted to immerse myself in the training as much as possible. The first week was like four hours a day of fight training; just stretching and going over the training with sticks and slowly building up to the lightsaber. Then I went to New York and worked with people they sent there. Whenever we're not on set, I'm always with the fight guys. It's almost like a play in a way, the dancing part of fighting. There's a structure and it's important to know where everything's going. You always learn new things about it, and for me this has been a process where a lot of the external things have been formed that gave me more information. Usually I feel like I try to work internally and try to think about how it feels from the inside out, but for this there are so many tactile things that I can actually hold on to that give me a lot of information. The fight choreography was one of them.

SITH STAR

FOR MANY, DARTH VADER IS THE DEFINING ICON OF THE *STAR WARS* SAGA. YET FOR ALL HIS PRESENCE IN THE ORIGINAL TRILOGY —AND HIS FORESHADOWING IN THE PREQUELS— IT TOOK A GROUNDBREAKING COMIC SERIES TO REALLY MAKE THE SITH THE STAR! WORDS: MICHAEL KOGGE

Star Wars Insider: *Darth Vader* helped kickstart Marvel's *Star Wars* comics line in 2015. How did it come to be one of the two launch titles?

Jordan D. White: One of the first ideas we had for the line was that we would have multiple ongoing series that happened simultaneously. It was definitely a departure from what had been done with *Star Wars* comics before, but it was much more in line with what Marvel does. When you buy comics for the various *Avengers* titles, they all take place together; and while they can be read separately, reading them together creates a richer universe. We wanted to do that with *Star Wars* as well. Once that idea was hatched, and it was obvious the main book would be *Star Wars*, and would follow Luke and the rebels. Darth Vader leading the second book was the natural next step. We followed Anakin's journey as a main character in the prequel trilogy, so it makes sense to keep following him into the original trilogy. There's a side of the character that we didn't know existed when those movies came out, but we had the opportunity to delve into it in a way that ties the two eras closer together.

Jennifer Heddle: When the series was in the concept stage I figured it would just be a fun read about Darth Vader kicking butt across the galaxy—not that there's anything wrong with that! But what Kieron and Salva made became much, much more. I realized by the end of the very first issue that this team was on to something special.

> ## MEET TEAM VADER!
>
> KIERON GILLEN, writer
>
> SALVADOR "SALVA" LARROCA, artist
>
> FRANK PARISI, senior editor, Lucasfilm
>
> JENNIFER HEDDLE, senior editor, Lucasfilm
>
> JORDAN D. WHITE, comics editor, Marvel
>
> HEATHER ANTOS, assistant editor, Marvel

What made Marvel decide Kieron Gillen and Salvador Larroca were the ideal team?

JDW: I thought of Kieron because of his amazing ability to write compelling evil. When Kieron wrote *Uncanny X-Men*, it was a dark time for the X-Men and, in my opinion, one in which they were close to being super-villains. Even so, he made Cyclops and company very understandable and interesting. In addition, his work on *Uber* for Avatar Press is literally re-imagining the darkest parts of the 20th century and making them even more horrific, while still telling an engrossing story. Both of those series mixed in my head and made me sure he could get into the mind of the worst villain in the galaxy.

Salva is a huge *Star Wars* fan; and the moment we got word that we were getting the rights for *Star Wars*, we knew we *had* to bring his amazing talent to the *Star Wars* galaxy. It was just a question of on what title. He's been able to capture the tone of the series so perfectly, from the first scene of issue #1 with Vader striding into Jabba's palace, right up through the last scene of issue #25 with... Oh, people might not have read it yet. I should hold off!

Kieron, how did *Darth Vader* enter your life? Is it true that you almost turned it down?

Kieron Gillen: One day I picked up the phone and it was Jordan. He asked if I'd be interested in writing the sister book to Jason Aaron's *Star Wars*. It was something of a surprise.

And yes, it's true I almost turned it down. The prosaic part is simple—I wasn't sure it would fit into my schedule. The more romantic part is that I wasn't sure I was the

FORCE IS OBSOLETE. THESE ARE ITS SUCCESSORS.

right man for the job. I was aware that Marvel had a lot of writers who would kill to do it! In the end, I decided I was as qualified as anyone, which is a terrible piece of ego. One of the main criticisms of my work at Marvel is paying more attention than I should to the villains and their motivations, but here that is a positive boon. For that and a bunch of other reasons, I realized maybe I actually was the right person for the job.

Salva, what was your reaction to being offered penciling duties?
Salvador Larroca: Surprise! A year before starting, Marvel told me they wanted me and it was a tremendous joy. But I preferred to be cautious until the scripts were ready. When they confirmed I was definitely going to do it, I was thrilled.

Was *Star Wars* a big part of both your childhoods?
KG: My first movie experience was seeing *The Empire Strikes Back* in the cinema. It was my entry into pop-fantasy culture; and Darth Vader was my first iconic image of evil. That I get to write the prequel to my own introduction to this world is the sort of thing that could blow a few fuses if you consider it too long!
SL: Yes, of course. I saw the movies as a child and I've always been a great fan.

I've always been fascinated by the character of Darth Vader. I'm afraid I've always gone with the villains! It is always more fun to draw villains than heroes—though in our story the Dark Lord is the hero, really.

What was your vision for the series at the start?
KG: When Jordan called it wasn't definitely a Darth Vader book. He told me if I had a better idea, go for it... But it was never *not* going to be Vader for me.

I viewed it almost like a historical novel because it's set in a distinct period in the saga. At the end of *A New Hope*, Vader is one of the few survivors to one of the biggest military disasters of all time, and he's at least partially to blame. But at the start of *Empire*, he's commanding the fleet, killing people at will, and generally has more power than ever. There's an implied story there—the fall and rise of Darth Vader—and that's what my arc would be.

The second key element, and the real emotional meat, is that between the two movies Vader realizes that he has a son. He realizes that the last 20 years of his life have been a lie. We had to do the inversion of the "I Am Your Father" scene—the "I Have a Son" scene.

I often use [the Netflix political thriller]

House of Cards as a shorthand description for the series: A powerful man feels slighted and turns to tactics he would have previously shunned to reach new heights of power. That core vision remained, though the execution always wanders. You knew in your heart of hearts that the final panel of Vader's story would be him, on the bridge of the *Executor*, about to go after Luke.

JDW: It probably won't be *too* surprising to hear that one of our major touchpoints in talking about this book would be was [the AMC drama] *Breaking Bad*. Even though the series is heavy with gut-wrenching emotion, it always found room for humor. I think Kieron referred to [the project] as a post-*Breaking Bad* take on Darth Vader at one point, and I think [he] is very right.

Salva, you've worked with several noted *Star Wars* scribes. How is Kieron different?
SL: Every writer is different, as every artist is, too. Kieron is very easy to work with because he is very visual in his descriptions. He is a very good writer and his scripts are fun, which is important for an artist. When you spend a lot of time with a story, you have to have fun with it, otherwise it becomes very hard.

Kieron, were you ever nervous pitching Lucasfilm some of your more... inventive ideas?

KG: Generally speaking, we had a "Don't self-censor" approach. Don't assume that Lucasfilm will say no; pitch it and let them say no if they want to. We wanted to test where the limits were, but we were never going to pitch anything that wasn't *Star Wars*. For me, *Star Wars* is very much in the space-fantasy mode. It's never been hardcore sci-fi, and that's its charm.

Characters such as the Mon Calamari cyborg Karbin have that wonderful "space fantasy" feel to them. What inspires these characters?

KG: I was trying to think of powerful archetypes that would work in the high-adventure mode that *Star Wars* runs on. That's where we get people like Aphra—fundamentally an ethically inverted Indiana Jones archetype—and Thanoth—basically the genius detective archetype, but an Empire loyalist. *Star Wars* is about these

big, powerful characters, and finding novel ones is a big part of it for me.

Jen and Jordan, did any of Kieron's pitches stand out as especially playful or inventive?

JH: The first thing that comes to mind is the mental image I got when I read Kieron's script about the Geonosian queen being hooked up to an egg-laying machine: "Only her top part is flesh.
The entire bottom half of her—the whole reproductive organ—has been replaced by a machine. It is basically the same shape as the organs would have been, but is clearly a machine. At the bottom, it has an egg-laying nozzle, but it's mechanical." I'm not sure "playful" is the word I would use to describe this, but it certainly is inventive! The suggestion of Triple-Zero as essentially a murderous C-3PO was also one of my favorite things. I knew it would work really beautifully and that fans would love it.

JDW: To me, the greatest and most joyful surprise was all the new and

charming characters that grew in the series. From the beginning, it was clear that Kieron understood the Dark Lord and had great plans for him. But all the new characters came to life on the page in such awesome and surprising ways. Doctor Aphra, Inspector Thanoth, Triple-Zero... They all became such compelling additions to the universe. In retrospect, I am pretty surprised we got away with making the evil R2 and C-3PO. They are actively psychopathic! It's pretty outrageous, but it seems like everyone at Lucasfilm loves them as much as we do, which is amazing.

Heather Antos: The new additions to the *Star Wars* cast have by far been the most pleasing surprise that any editor, creator, or reader could have. Kieron, Salva, and colorist Edgar Delgado's ability to bring such life to them has been astonishing to say the least. They've only been around for just under two years, but I now can't imagine the *Star Wars* universe without them!

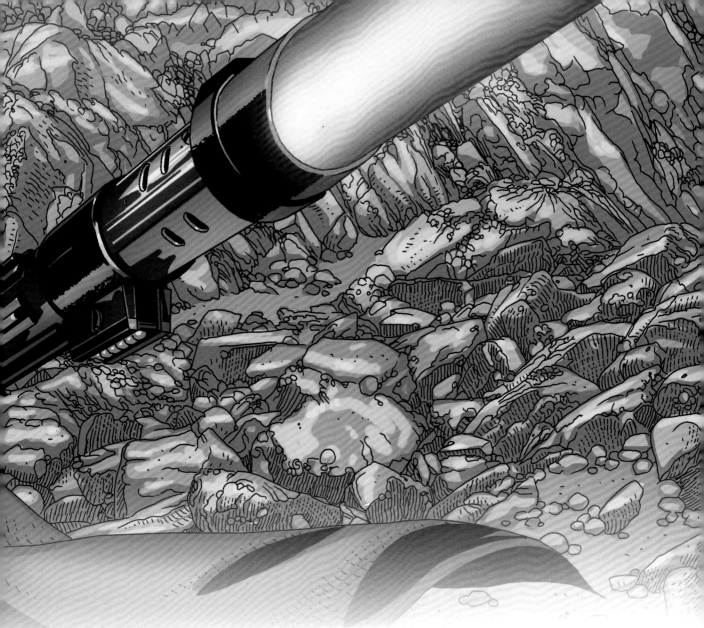

Issue #24 has one of my all-time favorite Darth Vader moments, and one that I was shocked we were allowed to do. It's a battle between Darth Vader and his former self, Anakin. Of course, it all takes place in Vader's head, but the fact that we get to see Vader's perspective on what went down on Mustafar—however skewed that perspective may have been—was super cool to do!

Salva, who were your favorite characters to draw, other than Vader?
SL: I love Aphra. She is special for me. And Cylo of course, because it's me!

Kieron, what's your process in scripting an issue? What makes writing *Star Wars* different from other Marvel titles like *Thor* or *Iron Man*?
KG: It's *Star Wars*. That sounds like I'm joking, but that is the key difference, and changes everything. I had spent basically the previous six years writing in the Marvel Universe. Though the Marvel Universe is a place with a large variety of tones, it still has a characteristic timbre. *Star Wars* has its own mode, and it's different. It's also narrower—which I don't mean as a criticism. Our aesthetic goal was always "We're not doing a comic adaptation of *Star Wars*, but we're doing *Star Wars* on paper." When looking at my choices when scripting it's always through the filter of "Is this evoking what we see on the screen? Is this *Star Wars*-y enough?"

In terms of the actual process, it's similar. I work on a script every day until it's done; I then leave it in a drawer for a bit before polishing it later. The secondary stage is when I hand it into Marvel, who then passes it to Lucasfilm for approval. The relationship there also changed things, and they've been generous with ideas and resources. At Marvel, I tend to write in a hermetically sealed way. For *Darth Vader*, there have been moments when I've written in the script: "I can invent a new crime lord here for this role, but if there's anyone in this area of the universe you're using elsewhere, I can use them instead." Leaning into the interconnectivity was a characteristic element of the job.

Also when writing for Marvel I'm less likely to stomp around the house, pretending I'm breathing through a ventilator!

What does an artist like Salvador Larroca bring to a panel? Did he find things in your writing or storytelling you didn't notice?
KG: Salva is a monster. My friend Matt Fraction and he collaborated on their award-winning *Iron Man* run, so I'd seen Salva's work extensively before—and also knew about his blistering speed. That last attribute is the easiest thing to overlook. He illustrated the entire *Darth Vader* series, thus ensuring the book's visual consistency. It's easier to lose yourself in a world like that.

I could see much of what made him perfect in the *Iron Man* run: he does brilliant technology, both in terms of drawing it and designing it. Aphra's *Ark Angel* ship has a great *Star Wars*-feeling design that's not based on anything in-universe. He also does fantastic likenesses, which is obviously a boon when doing *Star Wars*. All that was stuff I hoped for, and he completely delivered. Plus, he's an enormous *Star Wars* fan, which screams from every page.

Probably the most unexpected thing he brought to the page was basing Cylo's likeness on himself. It must have been an odd day at work drawing Darth Vader killing him over and over! It's probably a metaphor for working on the book.

Salva, how did you and Gillen collaborate? Might your pencils have inspired new directions in the story?
SL: I don't know if my drawings have been able to inspire Kieron, I just hope he's as happy with my work as I am with his.

When you work with such a good script, your obligation is to give the best of yourself to maintain quality. Kieron's scripts have been excellent and I tried to work as best as I know. When it's easy to work with someone, a symbiosis occurs, and that is visible in the result. I think that is what happened to us.

I got inspiration only from the movies, and it is important to the fans that the comic characters are recognizable.

Can you describe the challenge of illustrating emotion for a main character encased in black armor and a mask?
SL: I do it with body expression and camera angles. It's a trick that is used in films, too. It is not the first time I have to deal with a character like this. Think of *Iron Man*, for example.

Kieron, you've previously said that Darth Vader was your first image of "evil," since *The Empire Strikes Back* was the first film you saw in a cinema as a kid. How did you keep Vader evil, yet also sympathetic enough for readers to follow him through the series?
KG: It was tricky working out how to

present him without getting too close—and losing the essential mystique. That was something I worried about a lot. Our main solution was to show flashes of his inner life, but only at a distance. You'll have these single panels where you see a memory, but you can never be sure what the memory actually means to Vader. Plus, Salva and I really worked the "Silent panel of Vader staring into distance" hard.

In terms of maintaining sympathy, there were two main lines of attack. Partially it's that the story circles around Vader, and in some ways it's not *him* we're afraid of, but rather everyone around him. Have people we worry about

near him definitely helps there—Aphra is key to the book.

The other line is the absolute opposite: by surrounding him with people who are worse than him. Robert McKee argues in his book *Story* about *The Godfather* that one of the reasons the narrative works is that while the Godfather is monstrous, he's still a better option than anyone else. People find themselves thinking, *If I was a Mafia Godfather, that's the sort of Mafia Godfather I'd want to be.* I definitely did that. Vader is bad, but Grand General Tagge is bad *and* tedious. At least Vader wouldn't corner you in a party and talk to you about his favorite graphs.

I [also] knew the book needed a variety of antagonists. If [the story] solely consisted of Vader killing rebels people would quickly lose interest. I mean, isn't it telling that the moments in the saga we all love most are when Vader mercilessly kills one of his fascist subordinates?

As *Darth Vader* developed over many issues, did the story or the characters go in different directions than originally intended?
KG: Oh yeah. Many have been a delight. When I realized exactly what Thanoth was going to tell Vader, and why it was shocking, it was a real, "Dude! Are you actually going to do that?" moment. I spent considerable time wondering whether there was any way I could save him. Aphra had a bunch of scenes like that, and writing her desperately squirming to try and escape her fate was a joy. She always had an idea, and her scenes with Vader were always alive. That first happened in issue four, when I realized that the first thing Aphra would do upon completing the mission would be to ask, "So ...are you going to kill me now or later?" That unlocked the Vader-Aphra relationship for me.

The *Darth Vader* series also reveals that not every Imperial dies on the Death Star, as once believed. General Tagge returns in a bold new way to become a foil to the Dark Lord. Who made the decision to bring Tagge back into the fold?
JH: Using Tagge was a suggestion from Lucasfilm that came about during a meeting with Kieron early on. We wanted a foil for Vader who would feel like someone with a real weight behind him, someone that the audience would find believable as holding power alongside Vader and being in the Emperor's favor. Using a character from the conference room scene in *A New Hope* felt like the perfect solution. Everyone was excited about it. It was another bonus that Tagge was a character the audience no doubt already found obnoxious from the movie! You wanted to root against him from the start.

Kieron, how was it breaking story with fellow writer Jason Aaron on *Vader Down*, the crossover between *Darth Vader* and the *Star Wars* monthly?

KG: It was a lot of fun. All of this has been. I've known Jason ever since he was just starting *Scalped* and I was doing *Phonogram*. Also, we've had some experience in this kind of thing. Some of my fondest times in writing a shared superhero universe occurred when Jason was writing *Wolverine and the X-Men* and I was writing *Uncanny X-Men*. We batted stuff back and forth in a very casual way.

Vader Down was like that, but more so. We'd already done some close back and forth plotting on our first arc, building up towards issue six's "I Have a Son" reveal, but *Vader Down* was on a different scale from that. We had a variety of ideas, and our original thoughts for the series were miles away from where we ended up. It was a process of iteration, working on the synopsis, seeing where the issue breaks landed, and then just writing it. It was agreeably egoless in that way—we didn't even check which issue would be written by whom. As such, both of us got to write key scenes for each other's casts, almost by random. I'm still envious Jason got to write the initial fight between our two casts, though he's envious I got to write other cool stuff, so it evens out!

Why end *Darth Vader* with issue #25?

JDW: From the very beginning, Kieron always said this would be a finite story, that Vader is going through an arc, and that it would only really work if it had a conclusion. I am sure some will say we reached the end too soon, and a part of me might even agree—the part that just wants this team to keep making evil come true forever and always. But in the end, Kieron is right. The ending is an important part of this series, and it's stronger for getting there.

HA: Kieron has always had an ending in mind for the series. There was a story he wanted to tell, and he was able to do it in 25 amazing issues. I definitely wish the series could go on forever, but I think for a single story to have as much impact as this one has it *has* to end, you know?

Kieron, how would you say Vader's changed as a character from the first issue to the final issue?

KG: For me, it's a story of Vader awakening. Vader knows more of the truth now. As I said, he knows he has a son. Before this story the aim was to be the Emperor's fist. He's done that for 20 years. Now, at least consciously, he wants to seduce Luke to the dark side and rule the Empire.

Ironically, for all the darkness, this is

a story of a man regaining his hope and his own destiny. It's just a particularly dark form of hope, which has allowed him to act in an even more ruthless way than before.

What were everyone's favorite moments or scenes?

JH: There are so many! The invention of Aphra is obviously a standout—so many of the great moments in the comic derive from her being a fantastic character. I especially loved Aphra teaming up with the bounty hunters to rob the Imperial ship—all with Vader's knowledge. That was one of the most fun stories for me. I

loved the interplay within that group.

And I loved the cat and mouse game between Vader and Thanoth—giving Vader a worthy rival that actually kept me in suspense about who would come out on top! I think one of Kieron's real strengths on this comic has been surrounding one of the most unforgettable fictional characters of all time with other fictional characters whom you will never forget.

JDW: That is so difficult, as this is a series of amazing moments and characters. Right this moment, I will go with the character of Thanoth. He was so smart and interesting... and was a great

fans have been able to recognize the same Vader from the films in the comics. That is so cool because it's very easy to mess with such a difficult character to draw.

KG: Well, at least one of them would be in the last issue, and I wouldn't want to spoil that. Suffice to say we're really proud of the conclusion. I'm all about the denouement, me.

The first one is, I suspect, the one that would be on anyone's list. The "I Have a Son" scene. Salva paced it beautifully, and it's as iconic as anything that I've had my hand in while writing comics. It's a scene that any *Star Wars* fan would want to see, and I still can't believe I got to do it.

The second one would be issue 24. An issue-long vision quest isn't exactly what you expect this late in the game, but doing Vader's own cave-sequence-on-Dagobah worked shockingly well. We tried to make it mythic, and keep that sort of structure, and were very pleased with how it worked. If I had to pick one, while I was proud of the Obi-Wan and Anakin beats, Padmé whispering, "Stay" is one of my favorite panels in the whole book.

The third one... well, I can't pick between all the times that Triple-Zero and Beetee were monstrous and awful. I could probably do a top 10 of all the things the murderbots did. They were a consistent joy. And let's go with Thanoth and Vader's final confrontation. We did a lot of space epic in the book— obviously!—but sometimes all you need is two people in a darkened room.

Now, at its conclusion, how do you think *Darth Vader* stacks up to the other comics you all have worked on?
SL: At the top of my career.
JDW: Honestly, I believe in my heart that this will be remembered as one of the best Vader stories ever told. I think Kieron and Salva did that great a job.
HA: Kieron, Salva, and Edgar poured their hearts out onto these pages, and it really shows. I truly believe people are going to be talking about this series for a very, very long time come. How could they not?

antagonist for Vader precisely because he *wasn't* one. He was ostensibly on Vader's side, and it gave that whole second arc such a great layer of suspense—Vader is working with an investigative genius to solve a crime Vader had committed. Loved that. And Thanoth's return was also pitch perfect, if sometime we debated a bit about his final fate. I still hope, someday, we can read a murder mystery novel that takes place on the Death Star with Thanoth tracking down a killer in the Imperial ranks.
HA: Can I pick every moment that

happened between issues 1 through 25? *No*? Fine. In that case, my favorite moment was probably when we did the interwoven scenes between *Darth Vader* issue six and *Star Wars* issue six, when it was revealed to Vader that the troublesome rebel pilot was really his son, Luke Skywalker. I mean, what an *awesome* moment to reveal. It's such a pivotal moment not just for Vader, but for the entire *Star Wars* story as we know it!
SL: The sequences in which we tell Anakin's past, when we make a retrospective, based on the movies. That's very cool. And I am very happy the

Salva, would you ever take a trip down into the dark side again?
SL: I hope so, but who knows? I'd really love to. If I can, I'd do it.

Is this truly the end for Kieron Gillen and the Dark Lord of the Sith? Who was the master? And who was the apprentice?
KG: You strike me down and I will become more powerful than you can... wait, Darth. No, stay back. Let's talk this through—<thud>

Marvel Comics' *Darth Vader* series 1-3 are available now as trade paperbacks. ⊛

Star Wars Insider: How did you get started in the movie business? Was it something you always wanted to be involved in?

Brian Muir: I was offered an apprenticeship as a sculptor/ modeler at Elstree Studios in England. There had been 12 unsuccessful candidates for the position before me, but it turned out that I was lucky number 13. Having lived in Borehamwood [England] since I was two years old, I was very aware of all the film studios that were based there, Elstree being one. During my childhood, I had several friends whose family members worked in the studios and it sounded so exciting. But it seemed like a pipe dream to imagine that it would ever be part of my life.

How did you come to work on *Star Wars* and how was the project described to you?'

Arthur Healey, my mentor during my apprenticeship, contacted me to ask if I was available to start work on a new science fiction film at Elstree. All he knew was that it involved sculpting some futuristic characters from different planets and would probably be about six weeks work, but as it turned out I worked on the film for over four months!

SCULPT THE

BRIAN MUIR WAS ASSIGNED THE TASK OF SCULPTING THE ORIGINAL DARTH VADER ARMOR FOR *STAR WARS* AT THE AGE OF 23. LITTLE DID HE KNOW HE WAS HELPING TO CREATE AN ICON! WORDS: JONATHAN WILKINS

Can you talk about the process involved in creating Darth Vader from Ralph McQuarrie's original design?
The process started with Dave Prowse being molded from head to toe so that a full plaster cast could be produced for me to work on. As the mask and helmet were to be sculpted first, the head and shoulders were cut from the body and fixed onto a modeling stand. I began by sculpting the mask, back and front, ensuring that there was at least a quarter inch of clay on the plaster head at any point to allow for casting thickness, and to be sure it would fit well on Dave's head. After creating Vader's mask in clay, it was passed to the plasterers to mold and reproduce in plaster. I then carved and sharpened the plaster cast to a finish. At this point I started modeling the helmet in clay over the plaster mask to ensure the overall appearance worked. The same methods of molding and casting in plaster were again carried out. The final molds were made from the plaster cast, and

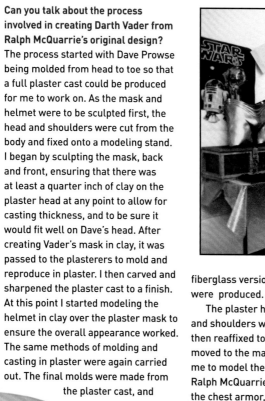

fiberglass versions were produced.

The plaster head and shoulders were then reaffixed to the body and it was moved to the main plaster shop for me to model the armor. Working from Ralph McQuarrie's paintings, I sculpted the chest armor, two shoulder bells, and shins. Again each piece was molded and cast in plaster, the lines carved and sharpened with a final remold, and finally cast in fiberglass.

Did this require you to work closely with John Mollo [costume designer], John Barry [production designer], and George Lucas?
I was asked to go to the wardrobe department to see John Mollo. He gave me

a simple line drawing without shading, at a three-quarter angle, of Vader's mask and helmet.

John Barry was the person who I worked closely with during the sculpting process. He came into my workshop each day to see the progress. It was John who suggested the "tear ducts" and the extension of the tubes past the mouth. In recent years, looking at the McQuarrie paintings, I've noticed the tear ducts were part of the design although they did not appear on John Mollo's sketch.

Although George Lucas came into the workshop a few times, he made little comment. Once John was happy that the creation of the mask and helmet were complete, he asked George to come into the workshop to give his approval. He seemed very pleased with the result and made no changes.

Did you work closely with David Prowse?
I didn't work with Dave—in fact I had no contact with him. I did see him on set on a few occasions, but the only time I've spoken to him was in 2006 when we were both signing at a memorabilia convention.

Is the approach different for a character who has a lot of screen-time (like Vader) compared to a character who is seen very briefly (like the Death Star droid)?
No, the approach is the same with every piece you're assigned. You do the best you can with whatever you're doing. It's the time constraints imposed by the filming schedules that dictate how much time you can spend on each sculpt, which sometimes reflects in the quality you are able to achieve.

How much creative input did you have on the finished sculpt?
With any sculpt taken from a two-dimensional drawing there is always some creative input from the sculptor. Every sculptor has his or her own personal style and own interpretations of a design.

How long did it take to sculpt the full Vader costume?
I probably spent five weeks total on Vader. During that time, I was also working on other characters. As the plasterers molded and cast different parts in plaster, I would sharpen them up for remolding and producing the final pieces in fiberglass.

How many Vader helmets were made for the first movie?
There were two finished helmets that were used for the production. They were kept in a locked box that was wheeled onto the stage by the wardrobe department each day. There was also a third helmet produced for the special effects department.

THE OTHER VADER!
By John Brosio and Pete Vilmur

If you're one of the lucky fans to snag a rare pre-release copy of *The Complete Vader* book, you may have been intrigued by the Darth Vader costume depicted on page 17—a costume that appears to have been based on early Ralph McQuarrie concept drawings for the character.

Often mistaken as an early prototype mock-up for the Dark Lord's helmet and chest armor, this was a Halloween costume fabricated by *Star Wars* concept designer Joe Johnston for a Industrial Light & Magic Halloween party in 1976!

Artist and former ILM Creature Shop employee John Brosio, who also happened to create a pretty stunning Vader of his own, recently asked Johnston about the fabled "McQuarrie Vader" costume, and its ultimate fate.

John Brosio: Did you construct the entire costume?
Joe Johnston: Yes, I made it in the model shop after hours. I put in one all-nighter as it got close to Halloween.

Was it styrene? Fiberglass?
It was slump-molded styrene over a fiberglass body mold that had been sent over with one of the costume shipments and discarded. The styrene completely covered the body mold which was a light brown and very rough textured. The helmet was based on a plastic German army helmet from the toy store, with styrene panels and model kit parts attached.

When was it made?
It was made for Halloween in 1976. It was based on Ralph McQuarrie's early illustration of Luke and Vader having their laser sword fight, which is why it doesn't look like the final version of Vader. The color is a blue gray, matching the illustration.

What became of it?
It was stored in a box of *Star Wars* things and was partially crushed when a box of heavier items fell on it as I was preparing to move to Marin County in April of 1978. It was too much trouble to repair so the entire thing went into the trash, except for the helmet.

Could you see out of it?
Yes, very clearly. I used a pair of tinted safety goggles as part of the faceplate.

Is it true that the costume never made it to Northern California?
True, except for the helmet. I saved the helmet for a few years, but pieces started to come off and since it really wasn't the Vader that the world knew, I didn't feel compelled to keep it from its destiny with the dumpster.

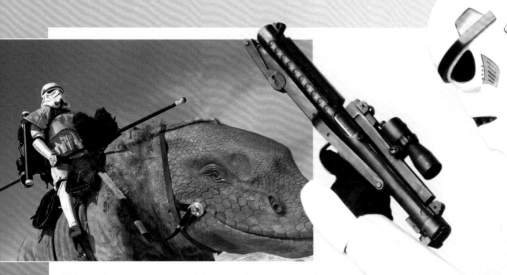

Did you also work on the C-3PO costume?

I did do some work on C-3PO. When I started on *Star Wars*, sculptor Liz Moore was just finishing C-3PO at the clay stage. She left the film to join her boyfriend in Holland at the end of January, 1976. It was then left to me to sharpen the detail in the plaster and add the slots across the side joints of the helmet. It was at a very late stage before filming that I was asked to sculpt the hand plates. There was no time to get a plaster cast of Anthony Daniels' hands so I had the unusual job of sculpting directly onto the back of his hands during the lunch break.

Can you tell us about your work on the stormtrooper costumes? Were they sculpted to fit a specific person?

The stormtrooper armor was the first thing I sculpted when I started on the film. I was given a plaster cast of an average-sized person. I began with the chest piece and applied the clay to the plaster cast. As I finished each piece it was molded and cast by the plasterers and, as with Vader, I sharpened the detail at the plaster stage. There were gaps between each piece to allow for movement so the stormtroopers didn't look robotic. Each piece mirrored the next so that it gave the appearance of a suit of armor but with gaps. The gaps allowed the armor to fit actors of varying sizes—the bigger the actor the bigger the gaps in the armor.

How much consideration is given to the actors? Is there ever trade-off between comfort and design?

Actors are given a certain amount of consideration, but the aesthetics of the costume are very important as well.

Originally there was a back and front to Vader's mask, which was sculpted and produced in fiberglass, but we realized that it would be claustrophobic for Dave, and the back was discarded. Also, to get some more airflow into the mask it was decided at a late stage to add a chin vent. I just drew this in the clay as a guide for the plasterers to cut in the finished fiberglass. Foam was inserted into the mask for a more comfortable fit. Unfortunately, the use of fiberglass does not lend itself to comfort.

Do you prefer creating costumes or set details, such as the space jockey from *Alien*?

I wouldn't say that I have any particular preference. The fine detail of whatever you are working on is satisfying. There is such variety in film work and it is usually interesting, although sometimes challenging. With sculpting the main characters for *Star Wars* there was a feeling of real involvement in the film rather than working on components of the sets, but from a pure sculpting aspect they are both enjoyable.

If you had the chance to work on Vader again, would you do anything different?

I wouldn't set out to do anything differently, but it would be difficult, even with a trained eye, to produce something that is exactly the same. The fact that Vader has become such an iconic character proves that it worked visually. ☺

ASAJJ VENTRESS
A-TYPICAL ANTI-HERO

TRICIA BARR ANALYZES
ONE OF THE SAGA'S MOST
COMPLICATED VILLAINS.

Often heroes are born of ideas, grand notions of saviors. Heroes must face down villains, the opponents over whom the hero triumphs along their epic journey. Sometimes, though, a story focuses on the arc of a protagonist who lacks usual heroic traits like nobility and selflessness—an anti-hero. The simplest example is Anakin Skywalker's descent into darkness in *Revenge of the Sith*; he is no hero as that chapter of his saga concludes. Since his tragic story unfolded on screen, many more anti-heroes have followed in his wake. One of my favorites is assassin-turned-bounty hunter Asajj Ventress, whose path to greatness was far from typical.

When the *Ultimate Star Wars* writing assignments were distributed, I was excited to receive some of my favorite characters, including Princess Leia, Ahsoka Tano, and Asajj Ventress. Condensing characters like Leia and Luke Skywalker, while intimidating because of their importance to the saga, actually proved far simpler than the ladies from *Star Wars: The Clone Wars*. *Ultimate Star Wars* is intended to serve as a summary of the canon events from the movies and television shows. Within that scope, both Luke and Leia have relatively tight character arcs that play out over three movies. Summarizing Ahsoka proved easier than Asajj, even though Ventress did not have quite the catalogue of episode appearances. The sporadic nature of her unfolding arc created part of the challenge, but so did the fact that Asajj Ventress started as an idea in George Lucas's imagination long before she became a fascinating piece of *Clone Wars* lore.

SMALL BEGINNINGS

Star Wars has a long legacy of characters evolving from small beginnings to become impactful participants in the fabric of the saga. The most recognizable example is Boba Fett, who began to take on a life of his own with the release of his action-figure prior to the theatrical debut of *The Empire Strikes Back*. From there, the bounty hunter's tale is the stuff of legend, or rather spread across a vast portion of the Legends stories as well as playing a role in the prequel trilogy and *The Clone Wars* television show. Other background characters, such as Aurra Sing and Bossk, have earned more affection from fans than was originally imagined for them. Asajj Ventress's origin is even more humble than a character developed to populate the world-building; she started as a visual that did not make the original cut during the movie-making process.

Concept art for a menacing Sith warrior can be found in *The Art of Star Wars Episode II: Attack of the Clones*. Villainous women were championed by Iain McCaig, also known for his designs of Padmé and Queen Amidala. In the book, McCaig discusses the creation process for the *Attack of the Clones*' new Sith: "I felt this was a great opportunity to introduce a strong woman character, to give girl fans an icon." While McCaig experimented with female Sith variations like a Padmé-inspired dark queen and a medusa-like alien, Dermot Power developed a vampiric, shaven-head warrior and martial arts-inspired alien with dual blades. This was not the first time a female villain had been tossed around in the conceptual phase; a fearsome Sith witch appeared in *The Phantom Menace* concept art. The Sith witch was set aside in favor of Darth Maul, and the female Sith warriors did not

make the cut for the second prequel movie, either. McCaig admits to being disappointed by the decision to move away from the female Sith conceptualization, but as with many good ideas in *Star Wars*, these striking designs would live to see another day.

Asajj Ventress was given a name when the artwork was fleshed out into a character (no longer a Sith) as part of the *Clone Wars* multi-media project from 2002-2005, which included the *Star Wars: Clone Wars* micro-series, books, and comics. It sought to tell stories within the timeline between *Attack of the Clones* and *Revenge of the Sith*, giving depth to the events that led to the fall of the Jedi Order and the rise of the Empire. The heroes of the Republic would face off with the conquering villains in Episode III, but as they moved toward their ultimate defeat, new foes were necessary to create surmountable obstacles, affording the heroes some victories along the way.

"A COLD-HEARTED HARPY"

Not every character in *Star Wars* will experience an arc, but when characters are used over an extended number of stories across multiple mediums, arcs can emerge. Asajj Ventress was a compelling presence. She had an air of mystery and danger. She dueled Jedi standouts, Anakin Skywalker and Obi-Wan Kenobi with confidence, delivering biting banter. A female warrior fighting Jedi men hinted at chemistry similar to ill-fated relationships that have arisen over the centuries in literature. While professional creators bounced Obi-Wan or Anakin against Asajj like flint to rock, fandom took those sparks and fanned the flames. While Ventress created electricity in stories from Gendy Tartakovsky's *Clone Wars* to *Jedi Trial* and *Obsession*, her personal story consisted mostly of being an adversary.

Asajj Ventress's arc started to shine during the *Star Wars: The Clone Wars* television show when writer Katie Lucas developed a fondness for the character. In an interview with ComicBook.com discussing the second trilogy of episodes she wrote for the series, Lucas revealed, "I've really fallen for Ventress, and here the audience gets to learn a lot about her history. She's an extremely complicated character." Calling Ventress a "cold-hearted harpy," Lucas set out to create a story where she finally "owns herself." With her powers growing, Ventress becomes seen as a threat to Sidious's machinations and her mentor, Count Dooku is ordered to kill her. Inspired by *Buffy the Vampire Slayer* and *Tank Girl*,

KATIE LUCAS SET OUT TO CREATE A STORY WHERE ASAJJ VENTRESS FINALLY "OWNS HERSELF."

GET TO KNOW ASAJJ VENTRESS

THE FORMER SITH ACOLYTE-TURNED-BOUNTY HUNTER PLAYS KEY ROLES IN SOME OF THE MOST EXCITING EPISODES OF *STAR WARS: THE CLONE WARS*. HERE IS WHERE YOU CAN FIND HER:

"The Hidden Enemy" (Season 1, episode 16) & *Star Wars: The Clone Wars* (movie) Asajj Ventress duels Obi-Wan Kenobi and Anakin Skywalker as she sets in motion the events leading to the Battle of Christophsis, then faces off with the two Jedi again after she has kidnapped Rotta the Huttlet in a plot to turn Jabba the Hutt's forces against the Republic.

"Ambush" (Season 1, episode 1) Ventress attempts to intimidate the Toydarian King Katunko from allying with the Republic, but her efforts are thwarted by Yoda.

"Cloak of Darkness" (Season 1, episode 9) Ventress liberates Nute Gunray from Republic imprisonment, and duels Ahsoka Tano and Luminara Unduli to a stalemate in her escape.

Lucas expressed an affinity for strong female characters in several interviews. She mapped that sensibility into Ventress's storyline in *The Clone Wars*, describing the character as an expression of "visceral female rage."

Since around the turn of the century, fan academics have been extolling the influence of *Buffy the Vampire Slayer* on pop culture at conventions and in scholarly writing in books like *Fan Phenomena: Buffy the Vampire Slayer*. With *Buffy* showrunner Joss Whedon now helming superhero blockbusters and writer Jane Espenson branching out to shows like the ABC hit drama *Once Upon a Time*, the relevance of *Buffy the Vampire Slayer* on the direction of popular storytelling may continue to be a topic for many years to come. The long-running arcs of characters like Cordelia, Faith, Drusilla, and Glory created roadmaps for future storytellers to understand that female characters do not have to all be likeable or good in order for an audience to root for them. *Buffy* and *Tank Girl* inspired Katie Lucas to take a villain, one who could have remained a sort of pastiche of the female bad girl, and elevate her to the status of anti-heroine, a character who might do bad things, but the audience still hopes she prevails.

"ARC Troopers" (Season 3, episode 2)
While General Grievous's droid army invades Kamino to strike at the Republic's critical cloning facilities, Ventress's task is to steal the original Jango Fett genetic sample. She nearly succeeds, but Anakin stops her.

A HERO REVEALED?

Over the course of *The Clone Wars*' run, Ventress crosses paths with a character spawned from the early Sith witch concept art, Nightsister leader Mother Talzin. A complicated history is woven between the two formative women that shapes our understanding of Ventress, who had been born a Nightsister and offered up to a criminal in order to protect the future of the matriarchal clan. In her backstory the classic elements of a hero archetype begin to appear, which might not be surprising given Katie Lucas's mentor was her father, George Lucas.

So who is Asajj Ventress? She is a Nightsister sacrificed to slavery as a child, then saved and trained by a Jedi mentor she eventually loses. Where Luke had a mentor and friends to keep his path firmly entrenched in the light side, Ventress is left alone and gives in to dark side temptations. As Sith do, Count Dooku exploits her abilities for his own gain, and the audience really gets to see glimpses of her true self as she is reborn a Nightsister. Unlike the compact arcs of the movies, *The Clone Wars* gave Asajj Ventress the chance to follow in the footsteps of Luke Skywalker, Anakin Skywalker, and even Buffy Summers; Ventress experiences multiple character journey cycles, peeling back yet more layers over the course of the television series. What we do know is that finding a family in the Nightsisters would be short-lived, and Dooku's retribution would cause Asajj to be left alone, yet again, when her clan is slaughtered by General Grievous's army.

From there, we have clues of Asajj's new path. Embarking on a life as a bounty hunter, her empathy for fugitive Jedi Ahsoka Tano leads

ASAJJ VENTRESS'S PATH THUS FAR LEADS TO A FORK IN THE ROAD.

"Nightsisters," "Monster" & "Witches of the Mist" (Season 3, episodes 12-14)
Ventress returns to her homeworld of Dathomir, reuniting with the witch leader Mother Talzin. After a failed attempt to assassinate Count Dooku, Talzin's Nightsister magicks transform Savage Opress into a fearsome warrior to mount a second strike at the Sith Lord.

"Massacre" (Season 4, episode 19)
Dooku dispatches Grievous to wipe out the Nightsister clan. Despite the witches' best efforts, Talzin and Ventress are the only survivors.

"Bounty" (Season 4, episode 20)
Following a new path as a bounty hunter, Ventress joins a crew assembled by Boba Fett to undertake a subterranean transport mission.

to a remarkable turn of events when Ventress allies with the Padawan, even offering critical information to Ventress's longtime adversary, Anakin Skywalker that helps clear Ahsoka's name. While the creative team on *The Clone Wars* had much more in store for the character, the show came to an end with a fitting heroic-arc style closure for its central character, Ahsoka Tano. At Comic-Con International: San Diego last summer, Dave Filoni revealed that Asajj's story would indeed be continued in the form of the adult novelization *Dark Disciple*, based on eight episodes written by Katie Lucas.

Asajj Ventress's path thus far leads to a fork in the road that has potential to branch in any number of ways. There could be a heroic rise or a tragic fall. Either way, *Star Wars* has done both paths exceptionally well, and it will be fascinating to see where the journey takes her, and the new shades she will cast in our collective understanding of how character arcs can create impactful stories.⚓

"Brothers" & "Revenge" (Season 4, episodes 21-22)
Maul and Opress wreak havoc in the criminal underworld. After they capture Obi-Wan, Ventress takes up the bounty posted by the Jedi Council and successfully rescues Kenobi from their clutches.

"To Catch a Jedi" & "The Wrong Jedi" (Season 5 episodes 19-20)
When Ahsoka is framed for treason, she flees into the underbelly of Coruscant. Ventress makes an unlikely ally for the fugitive Padawan, but she provides crucial clues that help Anakin clear his apprentice's name.

Dark Disciple (unproduced for television, released as a book)
A stunning new chapter for Asajj Ventress, proving that there is plenty of life in the sultry avenger...

THE
S

SULTRY SITH

CUNNING, DEVIOUS, AND MORE POWERFUL WITH THE FORCE THAN HER SITH MASTERS COULD HAVE FORESEEN, ASAJJ VENTRESS' TIME HAS COME WITH AN EPIC STORYLINE IN *STAR WARS: THE CLONE WARS*. *INSIDER* EXPLORES THE ORIGINS OF THIS INFAMOUS *STAR WARS* CHARACTER, AND MEETS THE ACTRESS BEHIND HER LATEST INCARNATION.
WORDS: JONATHAN WILKINS

ORIGINS OF ASAJJ VENTRESS

The distinctive look of Asajj Ventress came from early *Attack of the Clones* sketches by Dermot Power, who—along with concept artist Iain McCaig—explored a number of female Sith Lord concepts. As the script changed, this direction was abandoned and Christopher Lee was cast to fill the role of Darth Sidious' new apprentice, Count Dooku. McCaig and Power's concept sketches were filed and eventually used as the basis for a new villain that was needed for the *Clone Wars* micro-series in 2003.

The name Asajj was inspired by the character Asaji from Akira Kurosawa's *Throne of Blood*. Ventress originally was going to be named Juno Eclipse, but she underwent a name change to make her sound more villainous. The name Juno Eclipse was eventually given to the female co-star of *Star Wars: The Force Unleashed* and its sequel.

Ventress was first voiced by Grey DeLisle in the 2003 *Star Wars: Clone*

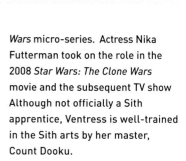

Wars micro-series. Actress Nika Futterman took on the role in the 2008 *Star Wars: The Clone Wars* movie and the subsequent TV show Although not officially a Sith apprentice, Ventress is well-trained in the Sith arts by her master, Count Dooku.

Alluring, cunning, and fiendishly clever, Ventress takes sadistic pleasure in tormenting her victims before killing them. Using her exotic magnetism, Ventress often distracts her foes before dispatching them.

She carries twin-curved lightsabers, given to her by Dooku, that connect to become a double-bladed weapon.

A flamboyant Force user, Ventress uses telekinesis and Force speed during combat, as well as the gravity-defying Force jump. Her skills with the dark side include the use of the Force grip, and the ability to control others' minds.

This page; Dermot Power's concept art that inspired the look of Asajj Ventress.

VOICING VENTRESS

Actress Nika Futterman has played the role of Asajj Ventress since 2008's *Star Wars: The Clone Wars* movie. "I just assumed she had a difficult childhood!" she tells Jonathan Wilkins and James Burns.

Asajj Ventress has grown even more powerful in the Sith arts since we last saw her. Have you approached playing her differently this time round?
Although she's back and more powerful, to me she is still the same person as she was before, and I'm playing her from the same place.

What are the challenges of playing Asajj Ventress?
I think the biggest challenge has been figuring out who she is. We didn't know a lot about her originally. The writers were creating her character as I was playing her, so I was coming from the same place as the audience, and asking, *Who is she?* I didn't want to play her just as a one-note character, because she does have a big history, and I knew we would explore that further down the line.

Were you aware of her back-story?
I had no idea about her back-story. The progression of the series is top secret, even to the actors! I always felt very free playing her, even when I had no idea where she came from.

"I DON'T CONSIDER ASAJJ TO BE TRAGIC. I STILL BELIEVE SHE HAS A CHANCE TO MOVE TOWARDS THE LIGHT."

I just assumed she had a difficult childhood, and that led to her feeling that she needed to prove something. Powerful people tend to come from backgrounds where they are making up for things they never had, searching for power, because they've always felt powerless. Learning about her past only strengthened the direction in which I was already heading.

Nothing surprised me in the storyline, it just showed me my instincts were correct.

Is evil fun to play?
Evil is the most fun to play! For me, most of my work is for kids shows and it involves playing funny and happy characters—so evil is the complete opposite of what I usually do.

Asajj has an all-new look this season. What do you think of her new threads?
I had no idea she had a new look. Like everyone else, I was psyched she got a new outfit!

Do you feel that she's a tragic character in a way? She's essentially punished for being

too good at what she does.
I don't consider Asajj to be tragic. I think if I played her with a sense of tragedy it would indicate there's no hope for her future. It would leave no sense of promise in her being. I still believe she has a chance of moving towards the light. She just needs to be given the chance. As for her being punished for being too good at what she does, you have to hate the game not the player! And she can certainly handle the haters!

Do you empathize with her at all?
I completely empathize with Asajj.

OTHER FUTTERMAN FAVORITES!

Like many in the cast members, Nika Futterman also provides voices of other characters. Remember Shaeeah in "The Deserter," and Chi Eekway Papanoida and TC-7 in "Sphere of Influence?" They're all voiced by Nika Futterman!

She's basically walking the galaxy alone, used, and misunderstood. She's lost all she ever cared about, and now the only thing that drives her is revenge. I think she's gotten to the point where she believes feelings mean weakness, and that's really sad.

Does she recognize the dark side in Anakin?

I haven't seen anything in the show yet that indicates her seeing Anakin's dark side, although at some point I know it will be impossible for her to not see it. Darkness sees darkness!

Would Ventress' actions make a formidable Sith Master?

Asajj is certainly capable of anything. Whether she curbs her anger is yet to be determined. Revenge can get in the way of anyone becoming a Master.

What's the most satisfying thing about playing Asajj Ventress?

It has to be her multiple layers. She could just be a kick-butt, sexy character, but she's also got a history and intelligence and most of all, shows no fear. Playing someone with nothing to lose leaves open endless possibilities. It's fun playing a part that I haven't fully figured out yet. This season is the first real exploration into why Ventress is the way she is, and it's really compelling!

What's the secret to being a great voice actor?

I think the great voice actors are the ones with the greatest imagination. Unlike being on camera, you actually have to imagine your environment. You also need to have a range where you can play somebody who's two or 92 years old, so listening to people and being able to imitate them is very important.

> "I THINK SHE'S GOT TO THE POINT WHERE SHE BELIEVES FEELINGS MEAN WEAKNESS, AND THAT'S VERY SAD."

Do you have a favorite piece of Ventress merchandise?

It's always incredibly exciting when one of my characters becomes an action figure! My favorite has to be my LEGO figure! That makes me feel like I've made it—the Asajj Ventress LEGO figure is just too cool!

Do you think Asajj could take down Ahsoka?

Oh yeah, definitely [laughs]! Asajj is very powerful, but Ahsoka's got so much heart, and she cares so much. I think it would be a great fight. We've seen some of it, and I think there has to be more. ☺

DECODING DARTH VADER

Following the rage-fueled appearance of Darth Vader in the Disney+ series *Obi-Wan Kenobi*, *Star Wars Insider* re-examines what we thought we knew about the Dark Lord of the Sith.

WORDS: MEGAN CROUSE

Obi-Wan Kenobi (2022) changed our perspective on some aspects of the saga that had previously remained unquestioned, while adding new layers to familiar *Star Wars* characters—not least of these being Darth Vader, the former Jedi whose turn to the dark side ran parallel to the fall of the Republic.

The series brought to the fore many of the things we already knew about Vader: his vengeful anger, his deep well of injured pride, and his belief in his own power. It also revealed new insights,

> "Mustafar was where we found this seething mass of broiling discontent at the beginning of *Obi-Wan*."

including the reason why Vader never traced his former master to Tatooine—Palpatine himself forbade Vader from pursuing Obi-Wan, ironically protecting the existence of his future nemesis, Luke Skywalker, from discovery. It also brought closure to one of the most important relationships in the Skywalker saga: that of Anakin Skywalker and Obi-Wan Kenobi.

Harnessing Hate
Vader was shaped in the metaphorical fires of the Clone Wars as well as in the physical flames that burned him on Mustafar. As a young man, Anakin had clashed against injustices, perceived or actual, such

01 More machine than man.
02 Darth Vader's reliance on his life-supporting armor and cybernetic additions was equal to the rage that sustained him.

as the reality that slavery and cruelty still existed in the galaxy, and the Jedi Council's refusal to confer the rank of Jedi Master upon him. His craving for justice twisted into an evil desire for control.

These facets in Anakin's makeup can be traced to events during the Clone Wars. His marriage to Padmé Amidala, for example, was pivotal in illustrating how his love descended into possessiveness and anger. Anakin's summary execution of the treacherous senator Tal Merrik also demonstrated how his moral compass sometimes went awry.

Having already adopted the identity of Darth Vader, Anakin's physical transformation into the cybernetic Dark Lord only magnified his anger. In the aftermath of

Revenge of the Sith (2005), as told in issue #21 of Marvel Comics' *Darth Vader* series, Palpatine's plan had come to fruition: Vader was fully loyal to the dark side, but the Emperor continued to stoke the flames of Vader's rage to ensure he remained so. Exploiting Vader's emotional turmoil as the Dark Lord settled into his castle on Mustafar, the planet where he had nearly lost his life, Palpatine planted an idea in Vader's mind that would ensure his protégé would not stray far. "Perhaps your Padmé does await you on Mustafar," Palpatine suggested. "Perhaps the dark side will bring her to you."

Thus, Mustafar was where we found this seething mass of broiling discontent at the

beginning of *Obi-Wan Kenobi*, a figure clearly under the complete control of both his Emperor and his own hatred. It is from this baseline that we can reassess the Vader we know from later in the Skywalker saga timeline.

The Rematch: Round 1

The brutal, unrelenting hate we saw emanating from Vader during *Obi-Wan Kenobi* highlighted just how much he would change over time. It's all too easy to think of Darth Vader as purely evil from the moment he donned the black armor to when he turned against the Emperor to save his son, but the character underwent a gradual, if self-interested evolution throughout the original trilogy.

When the Empire was on the rise, Vader's rage was all-encompassing, exemplified when he choked Admiral Motti for doubting the power the Force in *A New Hope* (1977). After his duel with Luke Skywalker on Cloud City in *The Empire Strikes Back* (1980), Vader became more contemplative, open to the possibility of a different path now that Luke knew who he was. By *Return of the Jedi* (1983), it was clear he was beginning to question whether he truly belonged to the dark side. Turning the clock back to the time of *Obi-Wan Kenobi*, however, Vader was still consumed by fury, emanating an aura of overt, intimidating anger, as we saw when he and Obi-Wan were reunited in battle on Mapuzo.

Faced with the unrecognizable silhouette of his former friend, Obi-Wan's response was to evade a confrontation with Vader for as long as possible, partly to give Tala time to get Leia to safety, but largely because he was horrified by what he beheld. "What have you become?" Kenobi uttered, his shock and confusion palpable. For his part, Vader seemed more interested in inflicting the same suffering upon Obi-Wan that he had experienced himself on Mustafar. "I am what you made me," Vader replied, adding, "You should have killed me when

03 Vader's calm use of the Force to choke of Admiral Motti was a hint at the anger burning within him.

04 Vader's true face revealed: a twisted remnant of Anakin Skywalker.

"When the Empire was on the rise,
Vader's rage was all-encompassing."

STAR WARS INSIDER / 67

05 Darth Vader, Dark Lord of the Sith.

"Vader showed no mercy, leaving the scene certain that he had finished Kenobi for good. That he had won."

▶ you had the chance." The ultimate expression of this was when Vader dragged Obi-Wan into a fire he had ignited from flammable rocks, intent on watching Kenobi burn as Vader had been burned a decade before.

This cruel, eye-for-an-eye act of vengeance was one of several mirrors between the two men in the series (note the reflective floor during their Coruscant training flashback). Vader recognized that the two were eternally tied, and, in his twisted way, wanted to make that comparison literal. Vader had consistently had the upper hand during the fight, almost toying with his opponent. The next time they clashed, in "Part VI," Obi-Wan needed to up his game. Fortunately, the Jedi Knight had changed over the course of the series, while Vader had not.

The Rematch: Round 2

Any illusion that Darth Vader was masking some internal conflict was

REVA: A TWIST IN THE TALE

Although Obi-Wan was the central figure in Darth Vader's life, *Obi-Wan Kenobi* added another character to the mix, further illuminating who he was: Reva Sevander, the Third Sister.

Vader had the power of life and death over each of the Inquisitors. That wasn't unusual for the Sith Lord, but what was unusual was that he had the power to promote or demote them, fostering a competitiveness amongst them. Vader essentially behaved as a manager. It was a microcosm of how he handled the Empire as a whole, controlling people through fear.

This led to one of the most dramatic revelations of the series: how close Darth Vader could have been to finding Luke on Tatooine, and closer still to capturing Leia and learning of her true lineage. If Reva had been as loyal to Vader as she had been pretending for so long, the fate of the galaxy could have moved in a very different direction.

dispelled when he and Obi-Wan fought again among the rocky spires of a barren moon.

During the fight, Vader almost killed Obi-Wan, attempting to crush his former master under a barrage of rocks from a position on higher ground, a reversal of fortunes compared to their fateful battle on Mustafar. On that occasion, the victorious Obi-Wan had left Vader to die in a pool of molten lava. Here, Vader showed no mercy, leaving the scene certain that he had finished Kenobi for good. That he had won.

This was not the end of the fight, however, and its climax had been foreshadowed in "Part V," in a sequence that took us back to happier times.

During a sparring session in the Jedi Temple on Coruscant, Anakin and Obi-Wan's practice duel neatly revealed their strengths and weaknesses. It essayed the complexity of Anakin's character— calm yet impatient, motivated by the deep well of emotion that seethed within him, and his capacity for both good and evil. Obi-Wan observed that Anakin was too eager to win. "Your need for victory, Anakin, blinds you," he observed. The same flaw continued to blind Vader years later. Even as the Emperor's right-hand man, he still suffered from the same egotistical need to win that Obi-Wan had noted. Having seemingly not taken his master's lesson to heart, the scene gave us leave to wonder whether

Anakin ever really become much more than a Padawan?

What we learned from those scenes was that Anakin remained a part of Vader, whatever the latter claimed. Vader fought in the same style in both eras, with forceful swipes of his lightsaber. Obi-Wan, on the other hand, knew that even in a practice bout a Jedi always needed to remember that their goal was "to defend life, not to take it." Anakin's response? "Mercy doesn't defeat an enemy, Master." Clearly, Vader held tight to this belief. Note that even when they were on the same side, brothers in arms, Anakin still viewed Kenobi as an "enemy" during their training bout.

On Jabiim, Obi-Wan took advantage of Vader's juggernaut attitude, to defend the lives of the Force-sensitive refugees and the Path rebels helping them. The need for victory linked Vader to Anakin in a very literal way. His eagerness to destroy the escaping ship meant he never considered it was a decoy. In the flashback, Obi-Wan snatched his friend's lightsaber, literally using Anakin's weapon against him. The literal move became metaphorical.

09 Darth Vader's Star Destroyer pursued Obi-Wan Kenobi to a barren moon where the former friends would fight once again.

One of the weightiest moments in the scene was when Obi-Wan handed Anakin's lightsaber back to him. It was an action of mercy and power—Obi-Wan could have won but chose not to. It is an echo of another moment in the Skywalker saga, when Luke Skywalker discarded his own lightsaber to stand before Vader and the Emperor without a weapon. More often than not, a Jedi's strength comes from deciding not to fight.

Through Tragedy, A New Hope,

Vader's sense of victory was premature, as Obi-Wan not only extricated himself from his predicament, but turned his full power on the Dark Lord, smashing his life support system and cleaving a gash in Vader's helmet and mask. The face revealed beneath was an abomination of the good man that Anakin had once been: Scarred, distorted by rage, and unrepentant.

In *Return of the Jedi*, Obi-Wan described Vader as "More machine now than man. Twisted and evil," and it was at this moment, during their fight on a barren moon, that he came to that realization. Given how the scene played out,

we can understand why the Jedi was so reluctant to tell Luke the whole truth about his father. The horror of what Anakin had become was too appalling to admit. The fact that he referred to Vader as "Darth" during their exchanges in *A New Hope* reads like a choice now, too. It was a decision, to deemphasize his relationship with Vader, and an acknowledgement that Anakin was long gone. When Vader declared that he himself killed Anakin Skywalker, Obi-Wan could literally see it was the truth.

Their duel in *A New Hope* can now be seen as the culmination of a sequence of tragic events, the final chapter in a once close relationship that carries the weight not just of the duel on Mustafar, but now of the two previously unknown encounters in *Obi-Wan Kenobi*. Vader had the upper hand on Mapuzo, as ultimately Obi-Wan did in the following fight. At the end of the series, the two were evenly matched, almost mirror images of each other in outlook and deed, with the result that their duel on the Death Star has more resonance than ever.

10 The final duel between Kenobi and Vader in *A New Hope*

MAUL

FROM SITH LORD TO CRIME LORD

Star Wars Insider explores how a combination of bad luck, bad timing, and bad decisions made the tattooed dark-sider the Zabrak he was.

WORDS: MEGAN CROUSE

Maul was trained to kill, his use of the Force always tending towards the easy aggression of the dark side. Yet some of the emotions that drove him should be quite familiar to us: fear, anger, and regret are just as potent motivators in our everyday lives as they are in a galaxy far, far away.

Maul might have appeared to be a straightforward villain, known as much for his dramatic appearance as for his habit of returning from the dead long after our heroes thought he was gone for good, but his storied life is an exploration of the consequences of bad luck, bad choices, and the skewed perspective of a villain who saw himself as the hero of his own story. Perhaps it is time to reassess the life of Maul with a degree of empathy he would no doubt never have afforded us?

The Unchosen Chosen One

As the apprentice in the two-person Sith hierarchy dictated by the ancient Rule of Two, Maul stood at the head of a line of dark-side legacy. Most apprentices grew up to attempt to (or succeed in) killing their masters, and Maul's life had been a contest from the very start, with Mother Talzin of the Nightsisters and Palpatine negotiating over the boy's fate in trials that left him disconnected from his blood family.

Once Palpatine took him on as his apprentice, the Sith Lord trained the boy to despise the Jedi. But alongside that hate, a jealousy formed and festered: if the Jedi made it their business to locate and adopt Force-sensitive children into their creed, why hadn't they sought him out? Maul's justification for this—surely to protect his own, mighty ego—was that he must

therefore be meant for a grander purpose. As Palpatine's apprentice, his status as a Sith embodied that thought, and became his sole reason for being.

During the invasion of Naboo, Maul was Palpatine's blunt instrument, a wall erected to deter Jedi Knights Qui-Gon Jinn and his Padawan, Obi-Wan Kenobi. The result was Maul's apparent death, but his "demise" in turn did feed a grand purpose: Kenobi became master to Anakin Skywalker, a boy destined to fall to the dark side and push the galaxy towards dominion under the Sith. Maul's assessment had been correct, from a certain point of view.

To look at these events from Maul's perspective, however, we can see this was his chance to shine that went terribly wrong. Qui-Gon Jinn was the first Jedi Master he had ever fought against, and Kenobi only ▶

01

CRIMSON FATE

Even at his highest point, Maul didn't have what he really needed: a family structure that wasn't put in place to manipulate and use him. Instead, he tried to build an empire that would protect and outlive him. Maul's two high points were both related to the underworld: first the takeover of Mandalore that put him in charge of both the planet and many of the galaxy's gangs, and his stint as leader of Crimson Dawn. On Mandalore, Maul had a throne and people who would enact his plans. Driven by fear himself, he drove others with the fear of displeasing him.

the second apprentice. In Maul's fervor to prove himself, he lost focus on the task at hand—the capture of Queen Padmé Amidala. Instead, he relentlessly pursued the Jedi because he felt it was his destiny to do so, thus paving the way for Anakin, the real Chosen One.

After his near-death failure against Kenobi, Maul sought out a family of his own, the family he had never had. Yet his spite and anger, along with his Sith training, kept him from achieving this goal too. Maul only knew how to exist using the tools that Sidious had equipped him with, making his relationship with his own apprentice (and brother), Savage Opress, cold and violent. When Savage argued that "There is no need for dominance between us," Maul shut him down and pushed him back into the "apprentice" role Maul was used to occupying himself.

During the early years of the Clone Wars, Maul was constantly trying to regain the attention of Darth Sidious and elicit the Sith Lord's good graces by demonstrating both competence and cruelty.

01 Maul and Obi-Wan Kenobi fought in several rematches during the Clone Wars.

02 Maul with his brother Savage Opress.

Everything he did was bait for someone else, including commandeering Mandalore's politics and killing its ruler in order to draw out Kenobi. In Maul's game of galactic chess, he was always trying to move others around the board, but he was never a master of Palpatine's skill, and instead his efforts were more akin to the actions of a child crying for attention.

Some of those cries had terrible consequences: Maul cruelly killed Satine Kryze just to goad Kenobi. While Maul argued that he could pit his gangs against Satine's "weak government" in the political arena, he was also still showing that he could only think within the confines of the small box Palpatine had constructed around him. Maul was no tactician; just a killer. And he was immature, always thinking of himself ("I will make you share my pain," he once said to Kenobi). As such, he simply couldn't comprehend the emotional bond between Kenobi and Satine, much less empathize with it. For Maul, their relationship was framed only as a tactical pawn to get him what he needed.

Eventually, Palpatine did respond to Maul's unspoken appeal, but still wouldn't give Maul the attention he longed for.

02

05

As the apprentice in the two-person Sith hierarchy dictated by the ancient Rule of Two, Maul stood at the head of a line of dark-side legacy.

Instead of welcoming his old apprentice back into the fold, Palpatine personally slapped both Maul and Savage down. Maul finally understood all hope of regaining his place among the Sith was lost.

Usurping the Darksaber
However, Maul was not willing to disappear. His ego and self-importance would not allow it, his vision of a grand purpose still central to his sense of self. He soon played a pivotal role in a conflict he would never have expected to have a stake in as a child: the Mandalorian civil war.

Maul didn't have any true claim to the Darksaber that gave

03 Duchess Satine Kryze was just one victim of Maul's quest for power.

04 Alliances, such as the one with Pre Vizsla, were mere stepping stones to Maul.

05 Maul soon turned on Viszla when the time came to secure the throne of Mandalore.

him the crown of Mandalore—it was built by a Mandalorian Jedi, not a Sith—but his possession of the weapon allowed him to prove to all what an important figure he should be. Eventually, this belief in his own heroic destiny backfired once again.

Maul believed Obi-Wan Kenobi would eventually come to confront him on Mandalore. After all, from Maul's perspective, they were fated enemies who had shaped each other's destinies.

Yet as the siege of the planet progressed Kenobi was otherwise occupied, dealing with a more important chaos agent in Anakin Skywalker—the Chosen One had begun to turn the wheels of the prophecy. Instead, Skywalker's

former apprentice, Ahsoka Tano, was the one who faced Maul on Mandalore (with the help of Bo-Katan Kryze, who had recognized her error in assisting Maul's rise to power on her homeworld), ending his reign. Once again Maul found himself cast onto the sidelines.

In a twist of fate, following Palpatine's enactment of Order 66 Tano and Maul were forced to work together to survive against clone troopers suddenly intent on ending both their lives. If Maul hadn't been captured by Ahsoka, he wouldn't have been in the right place to use his powers to bring down the ship where she was struggling to defend herself ▶

*STAR WARS INSIDER / **75**

LOWEST EBB

Half-dead, struggling to keep his thoughts in order, and raging against the Force, Maul's low point on the junkyard world Lotho Minor marked his journey beginning again after his defeat on Naboo. All he had left to him was the the dark side. His mantras—the Sith code and his own interpretations of it—reveal someone with deep anger, but also deep sadness. He felt unable to control even his own body, which he had cobbled together from flotsam and junk. Its flailing spider legs were stable enough for him to walk, but showed that he had become a chaotic, animalistic man after being abandoned by the people who had only used him to further their own gains.

07

▶ against an entire crew of clones. Maul was technically helping Tano, but she made a point of affixing no emotional component to the partnership. Like Palpatine before her, Ahsoka had pointed Maul at a target like a weapon, and it played directly to his skillset. After the ship went down, Maul disappeared. Ahsoka went on to become a key part of the rebellion against the Empire, while Maul seemed lost to obscurity. The Jedi never to be knighted

06 Maul and Savage Opress were no match for the power of Darth Sidious.

07 In later years, Maul found a potential apprentice of his own in Ezra Bridger.

by her own master found her own identity as a master to others. Maul's path was to become a dark reflection of her journey.

Being the boss of Crimson Dawn would not have been among Maul's aspirations either, but through it he served as a catalyst in the destiny of others: Qi'ra, who would become one of his high-ranking lieutenants in the criminal gang before taking control of it; Enfys Nest, an early rebellion fighter before the formation of the Alliance to Restore the Republic; and a space smuggler named Han Solo. It can be argued that Maul's truest destiny was to play a significant if unrecognized part in the journey of such important individuals, but this would have been a bitter pill for him to swallow.

From his very early life, Maul had believed in the appearance of a Chosen One.

08

Strange Mercy

From his very early life, Maul had believed in the appearance of a Chosen One. In fact, he was a believer before anyone else even knew about the prophecy. Although twisted, he had more faith in Anakin than the Jedi did.

That's why his ultimate fate, his jagged-edged alliance with Ezra Bridger, and his eventual death at Obi-Wan Kenobi's hands, was so poetic. Maul finally came face-to-face with his old enemy in the stark landscape of Tatooine. After coups and jails and witches, Maul's final moments took place in the simplest of places: by a campfire in the desert. In many ways, this wasn't even a duel of flashing lightsaber blades, but a conflict of personalities—Maul's clenched teeth and twitching eyes pitted against Kenobi's serenity.

In confronting Kenobi, Maul came close to disrupting a story bigger than even he knew. Maul sensed that something important pivoted around the boy Kenobi was watching over, and even as he drew his final breath, Maul was still focused on the prophecy. When Kenobi told him the boy was the Chosen One, his words offered some respite to the long-suffering Maul. After all, it meant Maul's predictions of the future had been accurate—he'd seen Order 66 coming, he'd seen the Chosen One coming. "He will avenge us," Maul whispered,

08 Obsessed with thoughts of vengeance, Maul searched the deserts of Tatooine for Obi-Wan Kenobi.

09 A final duel between the Jedi and the former Sith was over almost as soon as it had begun.

10 Maul's life was a rollercoaster of highs and lows, his aspirations forever being undermined by his personal demons.

drawing hope from an idea that Luke Skywalker would fulfill the machinations of the Sith and, finally, prove his struggles had not been in vain. Even with his dying words, Maul was unable to move on from his bitterness or the mistakes of his past.

Maul was the prophecy's most zealous adherent, and yet, everything

09

10

he did depended on his misunderstanding of it; reading from the source, believing in it, yet interpreting the situation entirely incorrectly. Not only was Maul not a hero, but he was also a study in how villains can show a dark side of perseverance, continuing to drive themselves with obsessions and aspirations that won't ever reward them. ☻

MATT LANTER THE ANIMATED ANAKIN

From swinging a pencil in place of a lightsaber to wearing retro shoes on a live-action set, Matt Lanter takes *Insider* on his *Star Wars* journey from *The Clone Wars* to *The Mandalorian*.

WORDS: BRYAN CAIRNS

"I actually had no idea I was auditioning for Anakin Skywalker," says Matt Lanter of landing one of the lead roles in Lucasfilm's animated series *Star Wars: The Clones Wars* (2008-2014, 2020). "They told me the role I was reading for was a character named 'Deak Starkiller.' I did a quick online search but there wasn't much out there, so I really had no idea. I remember Dave Filoni suggesting I give them my best combination of Luke Skywalker and Han Solo, and that's what got me the job. Obviously, there's a lot of Solo swagger in the *Clone Wars* Anakin, a lot more than Anakin in the films."

The show debuted as a feature-length movie in theaters in 2008, and ran for six seasons from 2008 to 2014, with a seventh and final season arriving on Disney+ early in 2020. Lanter, who is now 37, marvels that his *Star Wars* adventure has lasted so long.

"When I booked that job, I had no idea what was about to happen for the next decade and more of my life, and counting," admits Lanter. "All these years later, I have so many fond memories of working on *The Clone Wars*. My castmates, the producers, and everybody at Lucasfilm, they're like family to

01

me. I made lifelong friends from making that show."

Despite a six-year hiatus before the final season aired, *Star Wars* remained a constant fixture in the actor's calendar. "I've traveled around the United States doing conventions with my castmates, and this may sound cheesy, but the *Star Wars* fandom feels like family now too. I love going to cons and meeting fans who watch the show with their kids. There's so much in *Star Wars* to love, and it's so inclusive of everybody."

Set in the period between the movies *Star Wars: Attack of the Clones* (2002) and *Revenge of the Sith* (2005), *The Clone Wars* pitched Jedi Knight Anakin Skywalker and his comrades-in-arms against legions of battle droids, the Confederacy of Independent Systems, and the

02

03

ruthless Sith. Lanter took on the role originated in the live-action movies by Canadian-born actor Hayden Christensen, but the long-running nature of the television series allowed him to expand on his predecessor's take on Anakin.

"I went to Skywalker Ranch and sat down with George Lucas, and we talked about the character and where we wanted to go with him," recalls Lanter. "It was a conscious decision not to copy Hayden's performance. I would say there are influences, of course. Certain cadences and things like that. But I definitely did my own thing. I added more bravado. We made Anakin a little more charismatic, because we needed the character to take us through multiple seasons of storytelling. We wanted to show Anakin as this brave star pilot, this amazing Jedi, who was charming and funny at times. Hayden didn't get the chance to do that in the films, because he only had so many

> "I DID AN ANIMATED FEATURE ONCE WHERE I HAD A LOVE INTEREST IN THE FILM, BUT TO THIS DAY I HAVE NEVER MET THE OTHER ACTOR."

minutes of screen time to move his character from Anakin the bratty teenager to Darth Vader, the most hated villain of all time."

Into The Dark

Unlike live theater or on a movie set where multiple actors share a stage, it's often the case that performers might find themselves with only a microphone for company when recording voices for animation. It was a different matter with *The Clone Wars*, as Lanter explains.

"It's kind of weird. Sometimes you never even see your co-stars. I did an animated feature once where I had a love interest in the film, but to this day I have never met the other actor," he exclaims. "But with *The Clone Wars*, Dave Filoni loved to get all the actors together in one room. It was like an old radio play. We would go through each scene, maybe a couple of times, and then we'd move on. We would record a 24-minute episode in three hours. After that episode was done, we would spend half an hour on pickups for previous episodes. Maybe there was a slight animation change and the vocals needed to back that up. Maybe the showrunners thought the characters would be closer, but in the final animation they'd decided they were going to be 30-feet apart and yelling at each other. So, we would go back and pickup things like that."

The relationship between the voice artist and their microphone is not as static as one might expect. Lanter admits to sometimes getting lively and energetic in the studio, depending on what a given scene called for.

"I think all voice actors do things differently," suggests Lanter. "Some will sit down in their chair. Personally, I always stand up. I like to move a little bit, but I wouldn't be dancing about or anything like that. You can't really move off mic too much, but occasionally both Ashley Eckstein (who plays Ahsoka Tano in

01 Matt Lanter first voiced Anakin Skywalker for the 2008 *The Clone Wars* movie.

02 Ahsoka Tano (Ashley Eckstein) and Anakin part company in the 2020 final season of *The Clone Wars.*

03 Our last sight of Anakin Skywalker (Lanter), in *The Clone Wars.*

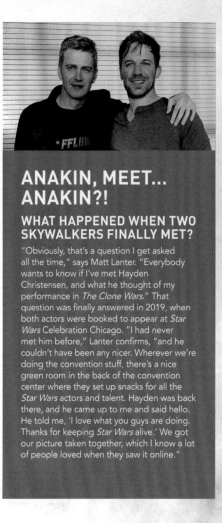

ANAKIN, MEET... ANAKIN?!
WHAT HAPPENED WHEN TWO SKYWALKERS FINALLY MET?

"Obviously, that's a question I get asked all the time," says Matt Lanter. "Everybody wants to know if I've met Hayden Christensen, and what he thought of my performance in *The Clone Wars*." That question was finally answered in 2019, when both actors were booked to appear at *Star Wars* Celebration Chicago. "I had never met him before," Lanter confirms, "and he couldn't have been any nicer. Wherever we're doing the convention stuff, there's a nice green room in the back of the convention center where they set up snacks for all the *Star Wars* actors and talent. Hayden was back there, and he came up to me and said hello. He told me, 'I love what you guys are doing. Thanks for keeping *Star Wars* alive.' We got our picture taken together, which I know a lot of people loved when they saw it online."

The Clone Wars) and I would grab a pencil if we had to be swinging a lightsaber around, in order to give our bodies some motion. You can hear that movement come through in your voice."

One such physical moment in the opening arc of Season Seven saw Anakin's darker side brought to the fore.

"I love those first few episodes with the Bad Batch," Lanter says. "I thought they were so unique and interesting, and so cool. And there was a great moment for Anakin, where we saw him get really angry at Admiral Trench, and then put his lightsaber through Trench's chest. I know that fans love those foreshadowing Vader moments, and so do I, because it offers that connectivity to Darth Vader and shows Anakin's dangerous lack of self-control.

"Dave and I were always very specific about those moments, about how dark Anakin was going to get," he continues. "Especially in the last couple of seasons, we were definitely conscious of saying, 'Okay, *this* is a Vader moment. We *are* going there. We *are* doing this.' They were done very purposefully. With Anakin, especially in the final season after putting the saber through Trench's chest and flippantly saying something like 'Have a nice day,' it showed his mood swings, his ups and downs. How he can suddenly turn extremely violent and then, two seconds later, he's back to being Jedi General Skywalker. I think that's so Anakin."

Live-Action Lanter

A few months before the final season of *The Clone Wars* was released on Disney+, Lanter made a surprise cameo appearance in Season One of *The Mandalorian*.

04 Anakin's darker side was revelaed when he threatened Admiral Trench.

05 Matt Lanter as Davan, in *The Mandalorian* Season One episode "The Prisoner."

06 Despite his on-screen death, Lanter was thrilled to make his live-action *Star Wars* debut.

07 Lanter at *The Rise of Skywalker* premiere in 2019.

He portrayed Davan, an ill-fated lieutenant in the New Republic Correctional Corps charged with guarding a prison ship packed with galactic miscreants. Forced to make a stand against a gang of mercenary infiltrators, poor Davan met a sorry end at the sharp end of a Twi'lek dagger. The role marked Lanter's first live-action appearance in the *Star Wars* franchise.

"Man, that was awesome. I'm so thankful to Dave Filoni for making that happen," says Lanter. "I got a call from my agent, and he said, 'Hey, *The Mandalorian* wants to know if you want to come down and do this thing.' I was like, 'What? Oh, okay. That's Dave! That's funny!' So, I texted Dave and said, 'Of course, yeah!' Who wouldn't want to do that? And it was great. I got to be on a live-action *Star Wars* set, actually inside a transport ship. I was like a kid in a candy store. It was awesome, and I'm really glad the fans loved it.

"It was an amazing experience for me to be there," Lanter adds.

COSTUME CONUNDRUM

WHICH IS COOLER, CLOAKS OR CAPES?

Voicing the animated version of Anakin Skywalker meant Matt Lanter never got to wear his character's signature Jedi robes, but that doesn't mean he does not have an opinion on the practicality of Jedi attire.

"Those Jedi cloaks are kind of cool," says the actor when *Insider* asked if he has a preference. "I'm going to say cloaks, because I've actually had to wear a cape for some parts, and sometimes a cape is *not* great in a fight scene. I have dressed as Obi-Wan Kenobi with a cloak for Halloween, though" he says, adding, "I already had a monk costume and repurposed it the next year. People still thought I was dressed as a monk, though."

04

"I KNOW THAT FANS LOVE THOSE FORESHADOWING VADER MOMENTS, AND SO DO I."

"I got to work with Jon Favreau, and, of course, working with Dave on live-action was cool in a different way. I've known him for years and years as a voice director and executive producer on our show. Dave is an amazing storyteller. He knows *Star Wars*. He understands characters. I went to visit the set once or twice when I wasn't working, and got to see him directing, and it was amazing to see him in this new environment, in this new role. I messaged him a couple of months ago and told him, 'Maybe it's kind of weird. You hired me, but I'm so proud of you and where you've gone, and to see all your accomplishments.' Dave has great things coming for him.

Lanter also enjoyed wearing his first *Star Wars* costume, a New Republic soldier uniform loosely inspired by the rebel trooper gear from *Star Wars: A New Hope* (1977), complete with familiar visored helmet, chunky belt, and disco-era footwear.

"My 70's retro shoes were awesome," Lanter laughs. "And Mayfield's line about them, 'Nice shoes. Matches his belt,' that was not scripted. That was something Bill Burr threw in there, and they kept it in. It ended up being a fun little extra moment, where they

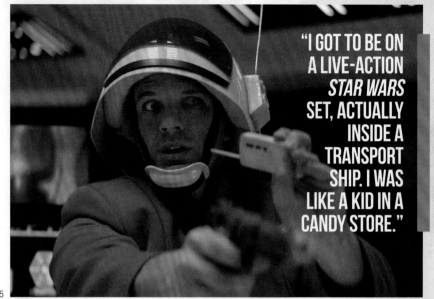

"I GOT TO BE ON A LIVE-ACTION *STAR WARS* SET, ACTUALLY INSIDE A TRANSPORT SHIP. I WAS LIKE A KID IN A CANDY STORE."

05

06

07

pan down to my shoes. I had a great time, although I couldn't tell anyone about it. That was the hardest part. As with all things *Star Wars* that I do, I can end up going a year and a half without telling anyone anything."

Despite *The Clone Wars* reaching its inevitable conclusion, finally synching with the events of *Revenge of the Sith*, Lanter isn't entirely prepared to hang up his lightsaber and say goodbye to the Chosen One. "I've loved working with Dave, and with the whole *Star Wars* family," Lanter concludes. "It's been such an amazing experience for me as an actor. *The Clone Wars* is perfection in my eyes. I'm certainly not ready to put Anakin away forever." ☻

Ian McDiarmid
Return Of The Sith

With his trademark cackle, the imminent return of Emperor Palpatine was heralded in the trailer for *Star Wars: The Rise of Skywalker* (2019). For actor Ian McDiarmid, it was a welcome opportunity to contribute to the completion of a movie saga that has entertained generations.

WORDS: MARK NEWBOLD

Ian McDiarmid first played the sinister Emperor Palpatine in *Star Wars: Return of the Jedi* (1983), returning to play a younger version of the character in the prequel trilogy that showed how the seemingly affable senator conquered the *Star Wars* galaxy through stealth and cunning. Having been killed off by Darth Vader at the climax of the original trilogy, as far as McDiarmid was concerned Palpatine's fate was sealed. Or was it?

Star Wars Insider: Were you surprised when the opportunity arose to pull on Palpatine's cloak once again for *The Rise of Skywalker*?
Ian McDiarmid: I was, because I'd assumed he'd been forever consigned to the galactic hell where he belonged. It really didn't look as if he was going to survive after Darth Vader shoved him down that shaft, so I was very surprised to get an email from J.J. Abrams' office asking for my phone number. When I eventually spoke to J.J., he said, "We're thinking of bringing Palpatine back. What do you think about it?" Well, my first thought was, "Hasn't he been destroyed?", and

J.J. explained that he's so clever, bits of him aren't the same as before, but the brain is still intact. So, I said yes, it sounded exciting, and indeed it turned out to be.

Once I'd read the script, and J.J. and I had talked about it, it all seemed highly feasible to me. As you see in the film, Palpatine was in a terrible physical mess, really knocked about and hanging up there in that strange contraption, but the brain was ticking over. In the original script he was much more badly mauled than you saw in the movie, which is probably just as well. One line I had that didn't make the final cut was when Kylo first encounters Palpatine in that first scene and says, "You're a clone!" My line was, "More than a clone, less than a man," which to me seemed to sum him up extremely well.

What appealed to you most about reprising the character?
The thing I liked was that he was so determined he wouldn't be defeated, that he would live on in some form, even if it wasn't going to be in his own body. That was a very interesting idea.

You'd imagine that someone with such a brilliant mind as Palpatine would think about the afterlife and not dying, and of course he implied what he'd ▶

"I'd assumed he'd been forever consigned to the galactic hell where he belonged."

▶ learned from his predecessor in *Star Wars: Revenge of the Sith* (2005), so I thought he'd probably have something along those lines tucked away somewhere.

More than that, I know J.J. felt honored to have the job of tying up these nine movies, and in a sense that honor was channeled through my character. When you think about it, Palpatine had been responsible, either directly or indirectly, for every evil act throughout these films, so it was a dubious honor to play him again.

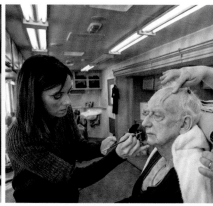

Along with the revelation that Palpatine survived, we also discovered he was Rey's grandfather. When was that plot twist first revealed to you?
That came out of the blue. I met with J.J., Kathleen Kennedy, and the casting director Nina Gold shortly after I'd agreed to do the film, and as I had a cup of tea J.J. went through the film and told me the plot as it was at that point, and he didn't spare any detail, he performed it. It was exhilarating to listen to. I felt like I'd seen the whole movie by the time he'd finished. It was an extraordinary notion to find out that I was Rey's grandfather, and sort of wonderful too. The films are full of fathers and sons, and now full of grandfathers and granddaughters

too, and it was a nice parallel to Kylo Ren's problems. We see just how closely Rey and Kylo are bound. I thought it was a brilliant stroke.

It was a very exciting day at Pinewood when we shot the scene where I tell Kylo that I'm Rey's grandfather, because as you may know, a lot of people involved in the process of making a film don't necessarily see a script. So, when we did the first rehearsal on set there was an audible gasp throughout the studio. I thought, "Well, if there's a gasp here and we can keep it a secret, there'll be a very big gasp indeed when the film is released!"

01 The Emperor's makeup chair for *Return of the Jedi* (left) and *The Rise of Skywalker* (right).

02 J.J. Abrams (center) directs McDiarmid, Adam Driver, and Daisy Ridley.

Much like the three trilogies, Palpatine's story played out in an unorthodox order, skipping from the middle to the beginning, then to the end. Has that been a challenge as an actor?
Performers in long-running television series only ever know how their character is going to develop from episode to episode, and that's not a bad thing. They suddenly find that there is a new aspect of their character that they can call on to play that they hadn't thought of before, and that was certainly true for me with Palpatine.

I didn't know that he was a young senator when I played the Emperor in *Return of the Jedi* (1983), and George never actually told me when we had our first meeting about the prequels. He said there were two people, the senator who was working his way up who would end up as the Emperor, and this other character. It was only when I got the call sheet for the first day of filming that I saw my number opposite a character called Darth Sidious, and I thought it was a mistake. Then I thought no, no, they don't make mistakes like this. It was only then that I knew I was two people in one. That was fascinating in itself.

That literal duplicity is at the heart of the character.
Yes, and I think it was really important for the story George Lucas was telling in the prequels that you should see someone move up the ladder towards the center of power using the levers of democracy.

These are a series of films primarily aimed at young people,

"Palpatine had been responsible, either directly or indirectly, for every evil act throughout these films, so it was a dubious honor to play him again."

03

and George was trying to relate to them the real world, showing how someone as clever and complicated and evil as Palpatine could twist and manipulate democracy while appearing to be in favor of it. It was very important to George to tell that part of the story.

Palpatine played a very clever, devious political game, turning the galaxy into his own ultimate authoritarian dictatorship. Of course, such figures ultimately fail because they're short termers, they don't really think too far ahead. By disappearing for so long and having various surrogates represent him, like Snoke who was genetically engineered by Palpatine,

03 Ian McDiarmid as Supreme Chancellor Palpatine in *Revenge of the Sith* (2005).

he was able to work obsessively to build this enormous army so that one day he could obliterate all opposition and move back to the center of things. It was an act of unqualified revenge, really.

Palpatine's problem was he couldn't be the person he was, which was the Emperor at the end of *Return of the Jedi*, until certain things were in place, which were all to do with the relationship between Rey and Kylo Ren, and we know how that worked out for him.

Speaking of Rey and Kylo Ren, you shared your scenes with co-stars Daisy Ridley and Adam Driver. How was that experience?
I was so lucky to be working with

two such brilliant actors. I spent a good amount of time with Daisy, and I would have loved a bit more time with Adam, but that was the nature of our scenes together. My first day on set was the first scene of the film, as Kylo Ren made his way through the caverns of Exegol and confronted me. The scene changed in all sorts of ways but basically the relationship stayed the same. It was about two characters experiencing danger at the same time, and that's always an exciting thing for an actor to play.

There are many great things about Adam's acting ability and versatility, but what really struck me was his amazing concentration, when we were close, eyeball to ▶

BACK IN A FORTNITE

The opening crawl for *The Rise of Skywalker* began with this chilling announcement: "The dead speak! The galaxy has heard a mysterious broadcast, a threat of revenge in the sinister voice of the late Emperor Palpatine."

But what exactly did that voice say?

Players of the videogame Fortnite, joining a *Star Wars*-themed in-game event just prior to the movie's release, were the ones who got to hear it. The Emperor's gravelly tones, performed by McDiarmid himself, sent this sinister message to the galaxy:

"At last the work of a generation is complete. The great error is corrected. The day of victory is at hand. The day of revenge. The day of the Sith!"

eyeball. I didn't know at that time they were going to replace my eyeballs (*laughs*), of course. He was wonderful to work with and just great to chat with. And he's so tall!

Daisy is delightful. She sings a lot before each take to get herself in the mood, which is great. She's got a very good voice, actually; she should do a musical one day. She's entirely concentrated but in a completely different way to Adam, and she was always worried that I might fall off or get dizzy when I was zooming in and out in Palpatine's contraption.

I wasn't worried because I quite like heights anyway, and I knew I was in very safe hands. There were four guys who were manipulating the contraption and the guy who was in charge could stop it at any time. I could stop it if I wanted to, but I didn't want to at all. I loved zooming around.

Was that contraption as uncomfortable as it looked?
We did a lot of fittings for the contraption. The original plan would have had me resting on my knees throughout, which would have been a little difficult as it would have put a strain on my back. That was so they could get closer to me for the close-up shots, but thankfully they discovered that they could do all of that quite happily with me just standing up and being swung around, so that's what we settled for in the end.

Palpatine is in pretty unappealing shape in *The Rise of Skywalker*. Was the makeup application very different to those for *Return of the Jedi* and *Revenge of the Sith*?
Interestingly enough, Lucy Sibbick, who was in charge of my face, and Martin Rezzard, who was in charge of my hands and other parts of the body, wanted to get close to what Nick Dudman had done for *Return of the Jedi*, because this is what the Emperor wanted to be again.

04 McDiarmid and Adam Driver prepare for Palpatine's first scene.

04

"In the end, we decided that he should be the Emperor that everyone knows from *Jedi* and I think that was absolutely the best decision."

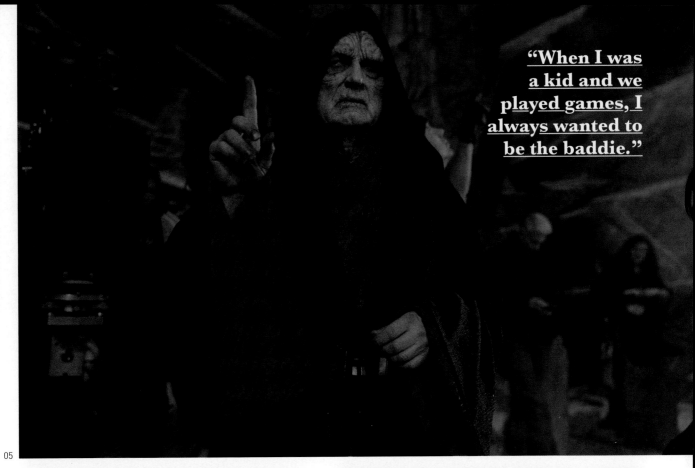

"When I was a kid and we played games, I always wanted to be the baddie."

05

06

07

There were discussions about what he would look like when he was returned to full power, and at one point it was thought that he would be much younger, which I would have been interested in, but in the end, we decided that he should be the Emperor that everyone knows from *Jedi* and I think that was absolutely the best decision.

I would go in every morning and place myself in their very talented and capable hands, and as it was with Nick, we started off fairly slowly and gathered pace as shooting went on. The first makeup, before Palpatine's power is returned to him, was like a theatrical make-up. I loved it. It looked very strange, even on set, and much as you see it in the movie. It was very odd and very pale around the mouth, like a face that had

sort of sunk into itself. Kind of appropriate. And the lighting by Dan Mindel was just brilliant. Later on they removed my eyes, though thankfully that was done digitally.

With Palpatine ending his days as a cloud of ash, what mark has he left on you?
When I was a kid and we played games, I always wanted to be the baddie, and when I started out as an actor those were the parts that were attractive to me. Many actors will tell you the same, because you can get your teeth into the baddies, so to have ended up playing the evilest creature in the *Star Wars* saga is weirdly satisfying.

It was exciting early on because

05 The fully rejuvenated Emperor Palpatine.

06 Palpatine exerts his Sith powers.

07 Rey (Daisy Ridley) confronts Palpatine in *The Rise of Skywalker.*

Palpatine was merely an ordinary politician. There was no apparent side to him, he was just doing a job and serving Naboo. I knew all the time what he really was and what he was doing, but it was exciting playing someone who appeared to be doing good while secretly practicing the worst possible kind of evil you could conceive of. That's what's great about his name—Darth Sidious. He's always insidiously, hideously there, throughout all the movies. That I could help finish off this great saga with that revelation, I could never have dreamt I'd be so lucky. In a sense it's been a series of strokes of luck. When J.J. called, I thought it wasn't so much a case of third time lucky, but lucky for the third time (*laughs*). ⚙

The Return of Ray Park

Maul's cameo in 2018's *Solo: A Star Wars Story* didn't just take fans by surprise – getting the call to reprise the role was as big a shock to Ray Park, the actor who first played him in *Star Wars: The Phantom Menace.*

WORDS: MARK NEWBOLD

When did you first learn that Maul might make a cameo in *Solo: A Star Wars Story* ?
I was on vacation in summer 2017 when an email from Lynne Hale (Lucasfilm's Vice President, Publicity and Communications) came through. I thought it was most likely to do with a public appearance, but my wife, Lisa, kept saying, "You'd better call her now, it's important." So I gave Lynne a call and that's when she broke the *Solo* news. I remember she said to me, "Remember, Ray, you can't tell anybody." Lisa was standing right beside me, so I asked, "Can I tell Lisa?" and Lynne said "No!"

Was it difficult to keep such an amazing secret?
I wanted to teach my kids the value of keeping a secret, so I didn't tell anyone—I didn't tell my wife, I just said cryptically, "It's a secret twenty years in the making, that's all I can tell you…" So she knew straight away. I'd said to my kids years ago that if I ever got that call again, Daddy would go crazy—in a good way. I'd have to focus, and manage every second of my day around training, and that's what I was doing. So my daughter was thinking, "Daddy's going to London in October; he's talking about shaving his hair; he's training all day; he's in the sauna at three in the morning; he's in the gym…" She figured it out.

I wanted to tell my Mom and Dad about it, but I was sworn to secrecy, so I just said, "Remember when I did something and I had to shave my hair? Well, it's something similar to that." I was wearing a beanie hat, covering my shaved head so as not to give the game away. For those eight months I was part of it, but it kind of felt like I *wasn't* part of it. All I wanted to do was get back into the make-up.

> **"For *Star Wars: The Phantom Menace* (1999), the make-up took about two hours to put on. It was nice and easy. It took four hours for *Solo*."**

Maul is older, and that's reflected in the way he looks. Was the make-up process the same?
The application was slightly different than before, because they wanted to age me; Maul's tattoos are faded, and he has a few blemishes here and there. But as soon as I was in the make-up, I was back in character. I felt like Maul.

For *Star Wars: The Phantom Menace* (1999), the make-up took about two hours to put on. It was nice and easy. It took four hours for *Solo*, and I had more people working around me because there were more things to work on. Everyone asks, "How can you sit there for four hours?" However, when you have music on, you're talking and having a laugh, four hours goes by really quickly.

Did you feel ready to return to the role?
I remember saying to my wife that I should be preparing, I should be pacing up and down, working out my different methods, looking at different options just in case, and she said, "You've been living this for the last 20 years. Just walk on set and do your thing."

Of course, I read my lines and made sure that everything was correct, but I wanted to have my mannerisms down because this was 20 years later; Darth Maul in *Solo* is a little bit different—he's matured, got a lot of baggage, and there's a lot more going on.

I had a lot of fun playing him in *The Phantom Menace*, but I was only 22 years old. Since ▶

PARK LIFE

Born in Glasgow, Scotland, in 1974, Ray Park knew from an early age that martial arts were where his future lay. Thanks to his father's love for the genre, Park grew up idolizing such greats as Bruce Lee, Chow Yun Fat, and Jackie Chan, in a decade that witnessed the explosion of martial arts movies as both mainstream entertainment and as an art form.

During his teenage years Park honed his craft as a professional gymnast and Kung Fu expert, competing in tournaments all around the world. He eventually decided to employ his talents for a different purpose and set his sights on a career in the movies.

After scoring a non-speaking, stunt double role in *Mortal Kombat: Annihilation* (1997), the big-screen adaptation of the hit video game, Park's career hit new heights when he won the role of menacing Sith, Darth Maul, in *The Phantom Menace*. The actor quickly went on to enjoy further success in blockbuster movies *X-Men* (2000) as the villainous Toad, then later as the iconic Snake Eyes in *GI Joe: The Rise of Cobra* (2009)—a role he later reprised in the 2013 sequel, *G.I. Joe: Retaliation*.

Park continued to add a diverse range of movie projects to his film résumé, including such projects as *Ballistic: Ecks vs. Sever* (2002), *Potheads: The Movie* (2006), *What We Do Is Secret* (2007), *Hellbinders* and *Fan Boys* (both 2009), *The King of Fighters* (2010), and *Black Box* (2012), while at the same time carving out an illustrious small-screen career for himself. The last decade alone has seen him steadily work through a string of TV projects including *Slayer* (2006), *The Legend of Bruce Lee* (2008), *Heroes* (2009-2010), *Spartacus: Blood and Sand* (2009-2010), *Nikita* (2011), *Supah Ninjas* (2011), and *Mortal Kombat X: Generations* (2015).

THE WAY OF THE WARRIOR

Recognized today as one of the best practitioners in the business, Ray Park began training at just seven years old to follow his dream of pursuing a career in martial arts. After originally specializing in Chinese Northern Shaolin Kung Fu (a traditional form of fighting known for its graceful fluidity and acrobatics), as a teenager he widened his area of interest into Wushu (Chinese Martial Arts).

The Shaolin discipline takes its name from China's Shaolin Monastery, where it is thought to have been originated by the resident monks around the time of the Tang Dynasty (618-907 BC). They incorporated spear and staff disciplines into the form, in addition to unarmed combat techniques.

There are 10 core classical forms—or areas of expertise—in Shaolin martial arts, and students train in them all, from entry level skills through to counter attacks, combat methods, close encounter combinations and many more. Characterized by kicking and leaping techniques (in contrast to the Southern Shaolin style which focuses more around punches and open hand strikes), rapid advances and retreats, aggressive attacks, and the whirls which Park employed to such great effect as Maul, the discipline also places great emphasis on speed and agility. It builds upon set routines which are learned and can then be combined as necessary.

The form was popularized by the late Gu Yu-jeung (1894-1952), who was responsible for unifying the many different styles of Kung Fu found throughout Northern China into the widely practiced and highly regarded Northern Shaolin of today.

Wushu—in which Park is an expert—is actually the term for Chinese martial arts; it's derived literally from wu (military) and shu (skill/discipline).

then my confidence has grown, I've gained more experience, and I understand how movie-making works, so I was able to get in there and really enjoy it. And Ron Howard was fantastic. He was unbelievable to work with!

How familiar were you with Maul's arcs in *Star Wars: The Clone Wars* and *Star Wars Rebels*?
I didn't realize that everything was tying in, that the comics and cartoons were connected to the movies. I didn't even think that Maul was going to come back for the animated series, and when he did I turned to my wife and kids and said, "He'll just be back for one episode and then they'll slice him in half again."
I watched *The Clone Wars* with my kids, and really got into *Star Wars* in that animated form. I loved it, and I remember saying to my son that with Maul appearing more there was always a possibility he could be brought back to live action. I'd played with my lightsaber and Bo Staff down the years, but when that storyline began I started to train harder!

How did you feel about Maul's eventual demise at the hands of Obi-Wan in *Rebels*?
I spoke to Dave Filoni, *Rebel's* supervising director, after I saw that episode. He said that everyone was expecting this big revenge battle, but I really respected what he did because, in my eyes as a martial artist, I felt it was appropriate. It honored the samurai movies that I grew up on. The characters weren't spinning around, doing flashy moves—it was very minimalistic because they were master craftsmen in what they did. One little error could mean death. Maul was being arrogant, and… Boom! With one strike Obi-Wan took him out. That scene meant a lot to me.

You've done lightsaber training events at various celebrations. How much of that draws on your own martial arts training?
Part of the reason I was cast as Maul is because I was trained in the Bo Staff, which is one of the hardest weapons to use as you're not only spinning it around, you're spinning it around

your body as *you* move in a big circle. I spent hours as a boy doing that spin you see me do at demonstrations and conventions—smacking my knees, smacking my shins, smacking my head, getting blisters on my hands… But what I'm showing is a basic move. That's a drill that I had to do thousands upon thousands of times when I was competing. With the Bo Staff you can move your hands up and down the stick, but with the lightsaber you're limited to the handle, so the style changes. I give it a bit of Darth Maul flair, and I do it with a lightsaber.
I can spend hours spinning it around my fingers, around my neck, and doing all of these different tricks. As Maul, I can use these tricks, but there's got to be a reason why I'm spinning it—not just to look flashy. There's a purpose to it. It's the lead up to another move. Recently I've been playing with some new moves and trying not to break my lightsabers.

> "Darth Maul in *Solo* is a little bit different—he's matured, got a lot of baggage, and there's a lot more going on."

To be able to perform at the level you do, do you need to be fully trained in martial arts?
What I tell everyone is: you don't have to know Shaolin and Wushu, you've just got to have a passion for *Star Wars*. As soon as you pick up that lightsaber you're going to feel like a Jedi or a Sith. No pun intended, but you're going to feel the Force. That's what I've done over the years—it's all Wushu and Shaolin techniques, but with a *Star Wars* flavor. That's what I love about all of these different saber guilds. You can have these fancy lightsabers and go and learn a kind of martial art because of *Star Wars*.

Would you ever consider going back to training others?
One day it may happen—if the acting doesn't work out for me, or I'm not a part of *Star Wars* anymore because I've gotten too old, I might start teaching and doing other things. Before all of this I was a martial arts and gymnastics teacher in London. But I'll do it because I enjoy it. All of the masters who taught me enjoyed teaching me.
I'll never forget traveling to Malaysia to train. I was taught for free, but it costs money to get out there, and my Mom and Dad ▶

borrowed so that I could follow my dreams and have that experience. I have that same mentality. If I train someone and I like them, I don't worry about it, there's no money involved—we'll have a cup of tea or a beer afterwards. My wife and my agent both say that I'm a terrible businessman!

What was life like before you got into films?
Busy. I wanted to go to China because I felt it was time for me to give up competitions and try and get into the movies, and I'd heard all these stories about film opportunities out there. But I didn't have any money. So I stacked shelves at a supermarket on the night shift until 3am, then I would go to the gym to work out. After that I'd get in my Ford Fiesta and drive up to the Hendon School of Gymnastics, sleep for a bit in the car, then teach gymnastics after school for an hour-and-a-half, go to Hendon youth center where I was in charge of all the recreational gymnastics up until 9.30pm and then back to

the supermarket again.

I auditioned for *Mortal Kombat: Annihilation* (1997), which filmed in England, and if it hadn't been for that then I wouldn't have been cast in *The Phantom Menace.* Had it shot in Australia, like *Attack of the Clones* (2002) and *Revenge of the Sith* (2005), I don't know if I would have been considered. I feel very lucky that I was in the right place at the right time and had the right people supporting me, including George Lucas, Rick McCallum, Nick Gillard, the casting director Robin Gurland—everyone was really supportive. It was great to have that feeling.

What has it meant to you to be part of *Star Wars*?
You know when you're growing

> **"I feel very lucky that I was in the right place at the right time, and had the right people supporting me."**

up, and your Grandad says, "You're a special one, something good is going to happen to you one day"? Well I was the kid who believed it—it gave me hope and determination. The thing that kept me focused was martial arts. It wasn't easy for me, but I loved it; I had a passion for it. I wanted to learn Mandarin, live in China, and become a Buddhist.

In 1982, when I was seven years old, we went to see a double bill of *A New Hope* (1977) and *The Empire Strikes Back* (1980). Vader scared me, but I was intrigued by Luke Skywalker and Obi-Wan, so I wanted to become a Jedi. I already wanted to learn martial arts, and was watching Bruce Lee films and TV shows like *Monkey Magic* (1978-1980), and *Kung Fu* (1972-1975), so when *Empire* screened straight afterwards, and Luke does the handstand with Yoda and his back flips, that completely changed me. I walked out of that movie house and asked my Dad for a lightsaber. I wanted to do martial arts and gymnastics and become a Jedi. It was the icing on the cake. *Star Wars* made it happen for me. ☻

THE LONG GAME

THE INSIDIOUS PLOT OF SHEEV PALPATINE

Insider uncovers how the machinations of a single, driven individual turned an entire galaxy on its head.

WORDS: MICHAEL KOGGE

The Emperor

...

In the 1970s and 1980s, the tyrannical ruler of the *Star Wars* galaxy had no further appellation. Though his surname "Palpatine" was mentioned in the novelizations, as was his former office of senator, few but the most ardent fans paid it much regard. The characters in the trilogy only referred to him by his royal title, and the films did not delve into who he was or where he had come from. The Emperor was simply the Emperor: the baddest of the bad guys, the devil of the dark side, the ultimate symbol of evil in the universe.

The prequel trilogy, however, demystified the saga's greatest villain, depicting Palpatine not as a one-dimensional monster, but as a multi-faceted character. First introduced as the senator from Naboo in *Star Wars: The Phantom Menace* (1999), Palpatine's evil stems from a very human ambition for power and the decisions he makes to acquire it. "What these films deal with is the fact that we all have good and evil inside of us and that we can choose which way we want the balance to go," writer-director George Lucas told interviewer Bill Moyers at the time of the film's release. Lucas is saying that evil is not a raw, elemental force: it is a choice. And Palpatine's choices are nothing less than steps in a master plan to control the galaxy.

The Art of Deception

. . .

■ Lucas describes Palpatine in his screenplay for *The Phantom Menace* as a "thin, kindly man." He is bright in both spirits and intellect, and offers what seems to be wise counsel to Naboo's young monarch, Queen Amidala. Nothing about him or his manners exposes any malicious intent. In all aspects, he's the consummate career politician: effortlessly charming, unceasingly good-natured, and cognizant of when to lend advice and when not. Although the political winds around him may be turbulent, he never succumbs to that turbulence. He is a man without drama, harboring a seemingly inexhaustible supply of patience. One might say he's boring.

Yet underneath his respectful formality and unassuming smile lurks a cunning and craftiness that no one in the Senate detects.

Take his conference with Queen Amidala in his quarters on Coruscant, for example. The queen has come to the Republic capital to implore the Senate for help in freeing her world from the Trade Federation's blockade. Palpatine is frank with her, saying there's little chance the Senate will do anything to

quash the invasion. In fact, he describes the Senate as "full of greedy, squabbling delegates," who only look out for their own constituencies and have no interest in the common good. Nor does Supreme Chancellor Valorum escape his criticism. Despite saying that the Senate's leader is "mired down by baseless accusations of corruption," and that a "manufactured scandal surrounds him," Palpatine advises the smartest course of action would be to call for a vote of no confidence in Valorum and push for the election of a stronger Supreme Chancellor. Without claiming any pretensions on the chancellorship, he in effect opens the door for his own election to that station.

Palpatine's counsel indeed moves Queen Amidala to address the Senate and call for a vote of no confidence in the Supreme Chancellor, which sets into motion Valorum's removal from office. An interesting line of dialogue not in the film, but appearing in both Lucas' screenplay and Patricia C. Wrede's junior novelization, shows the deposed chancellor's reaction to Palpatine's subterfuge. After his leadership

is thrown into doubt, Valorum turns toward the senator from Naboo and says, "Palpatine, I thought you were my ally—my friend. You have betrayed me! How could you do this?" The ghost of a smile that crosses Palpatine's face reveals where his true loyalties lie.

Palpatine's betrayal advances his own rise to power, as the Senate nominates him as Valorum's replacement. But Palpatine never confesses his designs on the chancellorship. Rather, he presents himself to Queen Amidala as a champion of liberty, willing to make the sacrifice to restore the Republic:

PALPATINE: "I promise, Your Majesty, if I am elected, I will bring democracy back to the Republic. I will put an end to corruption."

Palpatine does win the election to become Supreme Chancellor, proving that oft-quoted political maxim, "Never let a good crisis go to waste." Nonetheless, his ascent to the highest office in the galaxy is not his end goal, but only the first step in a grand scheme to take over the Republic from within.

BIRTH OF THE EMPEROR

A variety of influences can inspire an artist's creativity, and when it came to creating the Emperor, George Lucas was inspired by various sources. An avid student of history, Lucas drew upon the fascist ideology of Nazi Germany's Third Reich to serve as a model for the Empire and its Führer-like ruler. Politics during the eras when Lucas was writing *Star Wars* and its prequels also had an impact. During a 1981 story conference for *Star Wars: Return of the Jedi* (1983), Lucas was asked whether the Emperor was a Jedi, to which he answered: "No, he was a politician. Richard M. Nixon was his name. He subverted the senate and finally took over and became an imperial guy and he was really evil. But he pretended to be really nice."

In addition, one can't discount a documentary Lucas made as a student at USC in 1967. Titled *The Emperor*, Lucas' film is a portrait of Bob Hudson, a popular Southern California rock'n'roll DJ who appointed himself "Emperor" to his legions of young fans, and often costumed himself in robes and a turban. While the genre and subject matter are far from that of *Star Wars*, the imaginary title Hudson gave himself—and the film's title—might coincidentally have had an unconscious influence on the nomenclature and characters in Lucas' space opera.

The Great Fraud

...

Ten years after the Trade Federation's attempted takeover of Naboo, Palpatine remains Supreme Chancellor, while the galaxy is engulfed in a new crisis that threatens to split the Republic apart. The Confederacy of Independent Systems, led by the onetime Jedi Master Count Dooku, are rallying members of the Republic to secede from the interplanetary government that has held the galaxy together for thousands of years. Since the Jedi Knights cannot preserve law over such a large expanse, many senators want the Republic to build its own army, which it hasn't maintained for millennia. Others, like Senator Padmé Amidala of Naboo, who have lived through the misery of conflict, believe militarization will incite war on a massive scale.

Demonstrating why he's held the chancellorship for so long, Palpatine presents himself as a man of reason, sympathetic to valid security concerns, yet reluctant to disrupt the ongoing peace negotiations with the Separatists. In actuality, he's playing both sides against each other to amass more power for himself. He defers the mobilization vote, but when the Jedi Council learns the Separatists are assembling a droid army to attack the Republic, Palpatine agrees they must act. Senator Amidala's stand-in, Junior Naboo Representative Jar Jar Binks, convinces the Senate to vote to grant Supreme Chancellor Palpatine emergency powers so that he can move swiftly and commission an army on his own.

Palpatine pretends to be loath to accept such powers, going so far—in a scene in the shooting draft of *Star Wars: Attack of the Clones* (2002)—as to voice concerns to Yoda and Mace Windu before Representative Binks makes his case to the Senate. He says it's too extreme a situation, akin to a dictatorship. Yet that is precisely what he will slowly do with those powers: turn the Republic into a dictatorship, with himself installed as the sole leader. For the moment, however, Palpatine tells the Senate the opposite, promising that his emergency powers are only temporary:

PALPATINE: "It is with great reluctance that I have agreed to this calling. I love democracy. I love the Republic. The power you give me I will lay down when this crisis is abated."

With the new authority vested in him, Palpatine can do what he wishes without Senate approval. His first act is to create a Grand Army of the Republic, comprised of the clone soldiers whom Obi-Wan Kenobi discovers are being created and raised on Kamino. Years before, the Jedi Master Sifo-Dyas had foreseen that the Republic would be engaged in a violent future conflict and had secretly ordered the Kaminoans to clone an army of soldiers. Since Palpatine needs an army as quickly as he can get one, the clones are the most logical choice to fill its ranks. The Jedi agree to lead these troopers on the field of battle as generals.

The fact that clones and Jedi make up the Republic's infantry stifles public outcry. Citizens are encouraged to serve in the Republic Navy, but aren't being conscripted for combat, so no one has to unwillingly sacrifice their life to wage war on other worlds. This affords Palpatine a buffer from major political resistance during the initial stages of what becomes known as "the Clone Wars." Nevertheless, as he watches clone troopers board and take off in assault ships at the end of *Attack of the Clones*, he is clearly solemn and sad, as if this was a desperately unwanted but necessary evil.

In truth, Palpatine's plan has taken a giant leap forward, with the conflict throwing the galaxy into turmoil and bringing his goal of dictatorial power ever closer.

The Two Are One

• • •

◾ Palpatine has an ally who aids his climb. Some in the Jedi Council surmise that this mysterious figure may be the one behind all the galactic chaos, but they have not been able to locate him or confirm their suspicions.

The ally is a man of Palpatine's age, stature, and physique, yet instead of the ornate dress of the chancellor, he wears simple zeyd-cloth robes, with his face cowled under a hood. This man also has talents and powers beyond those which some would consider natural. His name is Darth Sidious and he is a Sith, one of an ancient order of devotees to the dark side of the Force. Though the Jedi believe they eradicated the Sith long ago, they have in fact survived: always in pairs, a master and an apprentice.

Over the last two decades, Sidious has spun his dark web, using his infernal powers to slowly, inexorably draw the Republic to the brink of collapse. He has turned Count Dooku to his side, appointing him as his apprentice and giving him the name Darth Tyranus. The two conspire to instigate the war between the Separatists and Republic, with the view that the Jedi will eventually fall and the Sith will re-establish security and order as new galactic rulers.

Sidious's greatest feat,

however, is that he does all this not by hiding in the shadows but in plain sight. For Palpatine's dark ally is none other than Palpatine himself. The mild-mannered chancellor with the calm demeanor uses the public forum of politics as his platform to bend the galaxy to his will.

Palpatine reveals his identity as a Sith to the Jedi Knight Anakin Skywalker, whose career he has watched with "great interest" since Qui-Gon Jinn rescued the boy from slavery on Tatooine. Sidious is in need of a new apprentice after losing his first, Darth Maul, during the Naboo invasion, and having his second, Darth Tyranus, decapitated by Skywalker. The young Jedi initially resists Palpatine's persuasions, but is eventually convinced of the corruption of the Jedi and the supremacy of the Sith. As a Jedi, Skywalker had not been able to save his mother from Tusken Raiders, but as a Sith, he can surrender to the dark side and potentially save his beloved Padmé from the death he's witnessed in his nightmares. Palpatine even convinces the young man that his wife may have ulterior motives.

PALPATINE: "These are unstable times for the Republic, Anakin. Some see instability as an opportunity. Senator Amidala is hiding something. I can see it in her eyes."

As usual with Palpatine, the truth of the matter is that he is not speaking about Padmé, but himself. He is the one who sees instability as an opportunity. He is the one who is hiding something. It is he who has orchestrated an all-encompassing plan that will soon reach its terrible climax.

Terminus

• • •

◾ Unbeknownst to the Jedi generals, Count Dooku had the Kaminoans implant a biochip into the brains of the clone soldiers. Upon activation, the chip would initiate "Clone Protocol 66," also known as "Order 66," which would force the clones to turn against the Jedi. After the Jedi who come to arrest him are killed, Sidious initiates the fatal order to clone commanders in the field, who in turn relay the order to their troops. The clone soldiers spin on their Jedi generals and fire, and in one fell swoop the order of brave knights that has guarded peace and justice for millennia is reduced to just a scant few. What the Sith have long desired—but never been able to accomplish—Palpatine has achieved: revenge against the Jedi. But he is not done yet.

With the Jedi Order finally extinguished, Palpatine executes the final step in his long quest for galactic control. He goes before the Senate and declares that the Republic will be reorganized into a new governmental body to ensure security and continuing stability. He will become the sovereign ruler, chosen for life. Thus the Empire and the Emperor are born.

The Long Game

. . .

◼ Palpatine is a patient villain, plotting his takeover for many years. Politics is his ladder, allowing him to make most of his moves in the public eye so that the sagacious in the Jedi Order never see the full picture of what he plans to do until it is too late. In the Jedi's defense, none of his choices seem evil on the surface; they are but political reactions to the direness of current events. Moreover, Palpatine's feigned hesitation to accept emergency powers or mobilize the Grand Army masks his true intentions. Boring, unimposing Palpatine represents that most ordinary malevolence, an evil so banal that it is inconspicuous, even to the man himself.

For the evil-doer never sees themselves as evil, demonstrating why even the most principled of men can convince themselves into perpetrating heinous acts. Palpatine merely wants to establish his version of security and justice, with himself as the final arbiter. Like his Sith predecessors, he believes the galaxy would be best served if it were under his command.

When Palpatine does announce himself as Emperor of the first Galactic Empire, it is, as Senator Amidala observes, to "thunderous applause." After years of war, senators and citizens cheer on their new leader, surrendering their liberties for supposed safety and security. But under this new Empire, that means oppression, domination, and blind allegiance to a New Order. As the minds of the citizenry become normalized to Imperial rule, soon even the surname "Palpatine" starts to fade in the public consciousness, until only a title exists: The Emperor. ✦

> **"Boring, unimposing Palpatine represents that most ordinary malevolence, an evil so banal that it is inconspicuous."**

NICK GILLARD

FROM CIRCUS TO SITH

Nick Gillard, the stunt coordinator who has trained more Jedi than Master Yoda, shares his memories of making the *Star Wars* prequel trilogy.

WORDS: MARK WRIGHT

Forty years after working on his first feature film, Nick Gillard is still one of the most sought after stunt coordinators in the business. Boasting a résumé featuring some of the world's biggest films and TV shows, his skills as a stunt performer have enlivened the heroic exploits of Superman, James Bond, and Robin Hood, to name but a few. But it was in the mid-1990s that Gillard's long-term association with Lucasfilm—thanks to his work on *Willow* (1988), *Indiana Jones and the Last Crusade* (1989), and *The Young Indiana Jones* Chronicles (1992)—led to him being approached by George Lucas and producer Rick McCallum to bring his expertise to the *Star Wars* prequel trilogy.

Gillard and his team were tasked with creating the huge array of stunts and lightsaber duels required for *Star Wars: The Phantom Menace* (1999), *Attack of the Clones* (2002), and finally *Revenge of the Sith* (2005), and he was credited as both stunt coordinator and sword master to highlight his work in these key areas. "Sword master sounds a little bit grand to me. I'm barely a walk master now!" laughs Gillard, whose career began when he literally ran away to join the circus and gained his first experience of stunt work. "Back when I was in the circus, we did medieval jousting tournaments," he

explains. "As a stunt person, you use all these little bits that you've learned. I'm certainly no master, but I know an awful lot about all kinds of fighting. I see myself first and foremost as a stunt coordinator, and I was involved in every stunt on those movies."

And there are *a lot* of stunts in a *Star Wars* movie, which one would assume places a huge weight of responsibility upon a stunt coordinator's shoulders. "It does and it doesn't," Gillard says, with a calm born of experience. "It's about how to keep everybody safe, so that you can shoot and keep the insurance company happy, and everybody goes home at the end of the day.

"Anything in stunts is achievable," he continues. "Anything at all. It's just down to time and money, but safety is the overriding concern. You're dealing with danger. I've just been risk-assessing a job I'm doing soon where we'll be shooting on a terrifying, 500-foot cliff with a full crew; we have a crane, the rain will be going sideways, and it will be blowing a gale. When you risk-assess something like that, it's something you really understand if you've been doing it your whole life."

The Biggest Show In Town
Rarely a day goes by on a *Star Wars* sound stage without some form of stunt work being required. Did that make for a very intense environment when filming the prequels? "It didn't actually. It was a lovely place," says

01 Qui-Gon Jinn (Liam Neeson) and Darth Maul (Ray Park) duel in *The Phantom Menace*.

> "I'M CERTAINLY NO MASTER, BUT I KNOW AN AWFUL LOT ABOUT ALL KINDS OF FIGHTING."

Gillard. "*Star Wars* is very unique in the business. It takes over an entire studio. If you go to Pinewood Studios, for example, there are often three other movies shooting, but when we did *Star Wars* at Leavesden Studios, we were the only movie there. You looked around, and everybody that you were working with had three or four Oscars. But [the first six films] were also independent movies. The guy that was paying for it all, George Lucas, was standing on set with you.

"You were part of a hand-picked crew, not necessarily because you were the best in the world, but because you were very good and you were going to get on with everybody so that it all worked," adds Gillard. "What that gave you was a lovely set. Yes, you understood you were making the biggest movie in the world, but everybody helped everybody else."

While Gillard's *Star Wars* work encompassed all the stunts on the prequels, perhaps his most prominent and visual contribution—one that still attracts attention today—was in bringing a new, dynamic style to the discipline of the lightsaber. The *Star Wars* prequel trilogy depicted the Jedi order in its prime, and sometimes in great numbers, requiring a specific approach from the sword master.

"When I do fights, not just in *Star Wars* but in anything, it's about tone, it's about knowing the characters," Gillard explains. "You have to read the script thoroughly and understand exactly what those characters are thinking in the moment, and why they're going to fight. You know who's going to win because you've read it in ▶

01

► the script, so you may have to disguise that or make it obvious, depending on the needs of the script. It's also key to understand the actor who's playing the part—their shape and how they move."

Gillard particularly enjoyed being able to eschew the strictures of real-world fencing and swordsmanship to craft fighting styles specific to the *Star Wars* galaxy. "That's what was lovely about the lightsabers; I could make up my own rules. It wasn't a defined thing where you could only do *this* move going in *that* direction. I made sure that I wrote the rules of lightsaber dueling first, so that it could fit anybody's shape or ability. You could teach those skills to somebody who was large or somebody who was small."

Across the three prequels, the lightsaber duels varied in scale, involving anything from two participants to several hundred. Gillard's flexible approach was therefore essential in coordinating major fight sequences, such as the climactic arena battle in *Attack of the Clones*. "We had to teach around 200 people for the arena sequence, and each of them was different," he recalls. "A lot of them were cast because of how they looked, but they'd never

swung a sword in their life. They had to go onto a sound stage on their own, in front of hundreds of people to do this fight routine, so we designed the duels to match their shapes."

Duel Of The Fates

The last act of *The Phantom Menace* features an unforgettable sequence that redefined lightsaber combat for a whole new generation—the balletic and furious three-way duel between Qui-Gon Jinn (Liam Neeson), Obi-Wan Kenobi (Ewan McGregor), and Darth Maul (Ray Park). "That's where we scrapped everything that had gone before," explains Gillard.

Like all the duels choreographed by the master stunt coordinator, this key sequence was being prepared long before shooting on *The Phantom Menace* commenced, and Gillard has nothing but praise for the commitment of the three actors involved.

"I've known Ewan a long time, and with anything you teach him, within a week he's going to be better at it than you are. I truly mean that," Gillard admits. "Everybody talks about Ray Park, but Ray's done this his whole life—that's what I brought him in for—and Ewan

02 Gillard describes the duel between Yoda and Dooku as "a very correct dance."

03 Gillard trained 200 people for the Geonosis battle.

04 The climactic lightsaber fight of the prequels.

had to learn it in three weeks. It was toughest on Liam, though. He'd done a bit of sword fighting on things like *Rob Roy* (1995), but he told me that *The Phantom Menace* was the toughest fight work he'd ever done. Ray was a gymnast—film work was brand new to him at that stage in his career—but he brought so much to it. The three of them together were perfect."

Spectacle aside, for Gillard the true success of a fight sequence always comes back to the story. "There's a through line," he says, "because Qui-Gon teaches Obi-Wan, and that leads on to Anakin. It's all in there."

From that defining battle between Jedi and Sith, right through to the

02

03

04

climactic duel between Obi-Wan and Anakin Skywalker (Hayden Christensen) in *Revenge of the Sith*, Gillard worked with a wide range of actors across the three movies, including Natalie Portman (Padmé), Ian McDiarmid (Palpatine), and Samuel L. Jackson (Mace Windu). "You were dealing with big characters, like Sam Jackson, the coolest man in the universe," Gillard smiles. "More than anything else he loves old Japanese samurai movies, but he didn't have a fight in *Attack of the Clones*. Mace Windu's duel with Jango Fett wasn't originally in the script. Sam sent me an email when we were prepping, which I think I've still got, that said, 'If you don't talk George into me having a fight on this movie, then I'll strike you down with great vengeance and fury and you will know my name is Mace Windu!' So we got him a fight. Sam loves all that stuff."

The *Star Wars* prequels' push of computer-generated imagery in films led Gillard and his team to work increasingly on fight sequences involving digitally created characters, such as *Attack of the Clones'* memorable showdown between Count Dooku and Jedi Master Yoda. Did that have an

impact on the stunt team's physical work? "None whatsoever," Gillard reveals. "Ours was a very correct dance. We knew where Yoda was going to be, and where he was going to jump—we even had a little maquette of him that moved around—so my guy could do his routine as Dooku, and he knew where Yoda was at every point in that routine. Then John Knoll and Rob Coleman from Industrial Light & Magic, who

loved the fighting anyway and spent a lot of time on set watching us, worked on Yoda—they did the rest."

Grievous Bodily Harm

A sprightly Jedi Master with a single lightsaber is one thing, but how much more complex did things become when one of the combatants was a droid Separatist with four arms, wielding no less than four lightsabers?

05

STUNT MASTER

Nick Gillard's route into the film industry started in the early 1970s when he left military school at the age of 12 and ran away to join the circus, where he became adept in bareback horse-riding skills. Gillard joined a group of fellow circus performers in providing horse-based stunts for the movie *The Thief of Baghdad* (1978), and from there a career in the film industry beckoned.

"I drifted into it by mistake," says Gillard. "We went from the circus to do a job, and there was so much free food! That was my main interest in becoming a stunt person. I really wasn't a film buff. I got on the stunt register at 18 years old—I was incredibly young and as brave as a lion. It seemed perfect. Just the same as being in the circus, dressing up and playing with friends."

Among his earliest film work as a stunt performer, Gillard worked on *Superman: The Movie* (1978), *For Your Eyes Only* (1981), *Krull* (1983), and *Aliens* (1986). "I was the Alien queen!" the stunt coordinator laughs. He also doubled for Mark Hamill on *Britannia Hospital* (1981), and David Bowie in *Labyrinth* (1986).

Over the decades, Gillard has divided his time between film and television with his company, Danger Inc., acting as a stunt coordinator and second-unit director on major productions. In 2008 he provided stunts for the action film *Wanted*, before deciding to work mainly on television productions, including *Da Vinci's Demons* (2013), *Jekyll & Hyde* (2015), and *Black Mirror* (2016).

▶ "We chopped those arms off as quickly as we could!" laughs Gillard.

"The General Grievous/Obi-Wan fight in *Revenge of the Sith* was a tough one," he admits. "We rehearsed with one of my guys on another one's shoulders, and Ewan McGregor had to fight with somebody in a boiler suit and

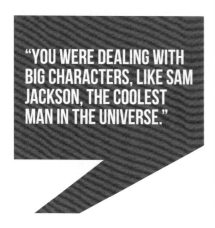

"YOU WERE DEALING WITH BIG CHARACTERS, LIKE SAM JACKSON, THE COOLEST MAN IN THE UNIVERSE."

a construction worker's helmet. There was this cardboard neck with a weird head on it that just looked ridiculous!

"People only tend to ask about the fights," Gillard continues, "but we did 100-foot falls, sideways falls, all of that stuff. The conveyor belt sequence in *Attack of the Clones* was brutal. Natalie Portman was fearless—braver than any of the boys. If it was written in the script, Natalie would be right in the middle of the action. She was more than capable and drove those sequences."

The Storytellers
Although ultimate responsibility for the action, stunts, and fights in the prequels rested with Gillard, he's keen to highlight the collaborative nature of his job. "Stunts and special effects are

05 Mace Windu (Samuel L. Jackson).

06 "Braver than any of the boys," says Gillard of Natalie Portman.

07 Digital combatant General Grievous.

08 Gillard as Jedi Master Cin Drallig.

always joined at the hip, along with visual effects. Those three departments are almost one group now," says Gillard. "And of course, I couldn't do without the stunt guys and the doubles working with me. Kyle Rowling, who doubled for Count Dooku in *Attack of the Clones* and *Revenge of the Sith*, still works with me. I gave him two swords when he came in to audition, and said, 'What can you do with these lightsabers?' Kyle did this great little performance so on the spot I asked him if he could start tomorrow! He's like another Ray Park, only six foot four!"

Gillard describes George Lucas as "his greatest collaborator," and easily sums up his experience of working with the visionary filmmaker. "He's the greatest, one of the best storytellers there is," Gillard says. "I think that's

06

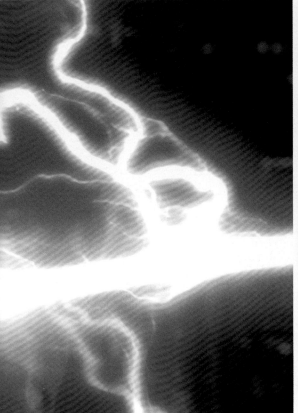

07

08

what he'd call himself—a storyteller, not a director or a writer, necessarily. For George, it's about telling the story. 'A long time ago, in a galaxy far, far away....'—straight away, you're into it. As a technician in the film business, that helps you believe you can do anything you want. It's very freeing."

After completing work on *Revenge of the Sith*—in which you can briefly spot the sword master himself as Jedi Cin Drallig—Gillard made a decision to focus on stunt work for television, relishing the immediacy of the medium over movies. "After *Star Wars* I did some of the smallest TV, because I had such a good time doing it. If I turn a car over on a movie, I can plan it for a month—if I do it on a TV show, they'll want it at 10.20 a.m. next Wednesday morning and we'll be done by 10.30

a.m. I might ask if I can go and recce it, and they can't afford it, so you've got to turn up and make it happen, which just keeps you alive and hungry for it. I promise you, at the moment I could not be happier!"

Busier than ever after 40 years of creating stunts for the biggest movies and TV shows, Nick Gillard looks back on the challenges of working on the *Star Wars* saga with great fondness and no little pride. "The movies mean everything to me, because they opened a door," he says about the saga's place in his life and career. "Everywhere I go, it will be the first thing I'm asked about. I'll sit on a train and hear somebody talking about the Darth Maul fight, or I'll see a kid wearing a backpack featuring a still from a fight I arranged. It's always there." ✦

FOOTPRINTS ON THE CRAIT SALT FLATS:
THE DARK PATH OF KYLO REN

Often the bad guys in movies are criticized for being one-note or flat, but the story of Kylo Ren is proving that villains can have an arc that is similar to the heroic monomyth. Tricia Barr examines the Villain's Journey of Kylo Ren.

WORDS: TRICIA BARR

Imagine Kylo Ren's story as reddened footprints stretching out before us on the salty surface of Crait. They represent the journey of Kylo Ren as it unfolds in *Star Wars: The Last Jedi*. If we turn and look backwards we can start to see more footsteps, the ones taken by the character in *The Force Awakens*. Further in the distance are subtle moments in time revealed through remembrances in *The Last Jedi* and by events covered in the novel *Star Wars: Bloodline*, written by Claudia Gray. Some of these footprints are blurry—stretches of his life story that remain hazy to the fans—but taking them all together we have enough to see the arc of Kylo Ren's Villain's Journey. The beats are the same as a monomyth, but instead of a heroic rise there is a tragic descent into darkness.

When we first meet Kylo Ren in *The Force Awakens*, his quest is revealed. He seeks the map to Luke Skywalker, that he might hunt down and eliminate the last Jedi. The conclusion of *The Last Jedi* brings the man once known as Ben Solo—Luke's erstwhile Jedi apprentice—to the pinnacle of this quest. The First Order assault force closes in to crush the fragile remnants of the Resistance, including Ren's mother General Leia Organa, inside an old rebel base. One man stands in his way— Luke Skywalker—who appears to have returned from self-imposed isolation. Kylo Ren marches out to defeat his former master, to destroy the Jedi, and their legend along with him. Everything that has occurred during Kylo Ren's Villain's Journey drives the emotional stakes to this climactic moment. However, before we can talk about where this journey takes him, we must go back to the beginning…

First Steps Into Darkness

A Hero's Journey can be marked by certain specific phases. So too can Kylo Ren's Villain's Journey. The Ordinary World for the Hero's Journey often reveals the hero to be a mere commoner, or isolated and unaware of their true destiny as a "chosen one." Rey's Hero's Journey fits the classical model in her introduction as a scavenger isolated on the desolate world of Jakku. Ben Solo is born into a life where his bloodline and mythic

powers are his ordinary world. The Rebellion, the fight against tyranny, the Force—these are what he knows and understands. What allows the audience to understand and identify with Ben Solo is a long established familiarity with the epic Skywalker saga—with all the *Star Wars* stories that have come before *The Force Awakens*.

The Call to Adventure occurs in the novel *Bloodline*. Ben Solo, who is off on a quest, training with his uncle Luke, learns that his grandfather was the evil Sith Lord Darth Vader. This shocking truth, exposed by Leia Organa's political rivals, unveils a secret Ben's family has hidden from him. While we can relate and empathize with the fact that there was never a good time to tell a child a truth that shames the family, most can understand the betrayal Ben Solo must have felt upon learning how deeply and how long his family had deceived him.

The Meeting with the Mentor— his dark side tutor, Supreme Leader Snoke—is obscured from the audience, but conversations in *The Force Awakens* make apparent that the First Order's Supreme Leader is the character who guided Ben's fall to the dark side. On D'Qar, Leia tells Han Solo, "It was Snoke. He seduced our son to the dark side. But we can still save him. Me. You." Later, when Han confronts him on Starkiller Base, Ren says, "Your son is gone. He was weak and foolish, like his father. So I destroyed him." Han counters, "That's what Snoke wants you to believe, but it's not true. My son is alive." Later Han asserts, "Snoke is using you for your power. When he gets what he wants, he'll crush you—you know it's true." The script states that "[Kylo] does know it," but perhaps the betrayals by his family in Ben's past prevent him from accepting that truth. Kylo Ren fulfills Snoke's wishes and kills his father.

Despite the initiating event of his journey and the arrival of his ▶

Kylo Ren marches out to defeat his former master, to destroy the Jedi, and their legend along with him.

▶ villainous mentor, Ben Solo resists the dark path for some time. He stays with Luke, and in remembrances from both Luke and Kylo Ren in *The Last Jedi* we learn that the darkness grew inside him as he continued to train at the Jedi academy.

The Crossing of the Threshold occurs on the fateful night when Luke enters Ben's hut and looks into his young apprentice's heart. For a moment, as Skywalker tells it, he considers killing his nephew as he lies sleeping, but he quickly decides against it. Ben wakes to see his uncle standing over him with a lightsaber lit, and instinctively defends himself. So, just as Rey's Hero's Journey starts in a fight for survival, fleeing Niima Outpost in the *Millennium Falcon*, Ben's path to becoming a villain in the galaxy far, far away is also influenced by a survival instinct taking over. His dark impulses stoked, Ben blasts Luke with the Force and leaves him for dead. He then destroys the Jedi academy, like his grandfather Darth Vader had pillaged the Jedi Temple on Coruscant as a fledgling Sith.

Testing A Villain

Many contemporary movies use the steps found in the Hero's Journey from Christopher Vogler's *The Writer's Journey: Mythic Structures for Writers*, which is a refined, modern take on the Hero's

01

Journey monomyth described by Joseph Campbell in 1949. Taken as a whole, *The Force Awakens* comprises the Test, Allies, and Enemies phase for Kylo Ren. This is the portion of the journey when the protagonist—in this case, Kylo Ren as the central figure of his own villainous arc, rather than as the antagonist in Rey's heroic adventure—confronts physical and emotional challenges, meets individuals who slow down his progress, and must decide who can be trusted. Each of these tests moves him toward a true knowing of himself as an individual. As expected for a villain in *Star Wars*, his allies, such

01 Kylo Ren corners Rey on Takodana.

02 As he attacks the Resistance fleet in his TIE silencer, Ren hesitates when given the opportunity to kill his mother.

as General Hux, aren't so much friends as individuals with mutual goals. At the beginning of *The Last Jedi*, Snoke makes apparent to Hux and Ren that they have both failed their tests as his underlings, as seen during the previous film.

Kylo begins *The Force Awakens* tracking down the map to Luke, but fails, owing to the efforts of new adversaries: "a girl," a droid and a defector. He pursues them to Takodana, where he unwisely leaves the planet without BB-8, based on his confidence he can retrieve the map from Rey's mind. His failed attempt to interrogate the scavenger only further awakens her latent Force powers, which then enables her to escape captivity. He passes his next personal test—killing his own father to cement his commitment to the dark side—and bests Finn in lightsaber combat before finding Rey to be a more formidable adversary than he ever expected.

In the Vogler model, The Approach to the Inmost Cave is the phase where the protagonist enters a special world and faces doubts. In *The Last Jedi*, director Rian Johnson creates a realm that is new even to longtime fans of *Star Wars*. The supernatural connection between Rey and Ren provides a means for the pair to converse with each other; to share some understanding and even sympathy. Ren confesses to Rey about the start of his villain's journey, and she reveals to him ▶

02

"IT WAS SNOKE. HE SEDUCED OUR SON TO THE DARK SIDE. BUT WE CAN STILL SAVE HIM. ME. YOU."

LEIA ORGANA

KYLO AND CAMPBELL

A PRACTICAL GUIDE

Christopher Vogler's Hero's Journey formula has been the go-to model of filmmakers since the 1980s, when his memo "A Practical Guide to The Hero With a Thousand Faces" condensed and modernized Joseph Campbell's historically focused monomythic model. But elements of classical mythology continue to appear in fresh new stories, often with a twist that reflects current trends in the world they are written. Some of the Campbellian elements found in Kylo Ren's Villain's Journey include Meeting with the Goddess and Woman as Temptress.

MEETING WITH THE GODDESS

Campbell describes The Meeting with the Goddess as an event where the hero meets a powerful female figure that gives him the support or information needed for his quest. In *A New Hope,* Luke meets Leia; in *The Force Awakens,* Rey meets Maz Kanata. Often in stories studied by Campbell, the Goddess offers unconditional love. For a villain, heroic tropes are twisted; for Ren, this support takes the form of conditions he must meet in order to earn the "love" of a powerful male figure, Snoke.

WOMAN AS TEMPTRESS

In *The Force Awakens,* Ren is distracted by the woman who flies the *Millennium Falcon.* Rey is the Temptress that lures Ren away from his quest to find and kill Luke Skywalker. If he hadn't abducted her and awakened her Force powers, things might have gone differently. In *The Last Jedi,* Rey stands before Kylo Ren in Snoke's Throne Room, asking him to join her to save the remnants of the Resistance fleet that is being destroyed by the First Order. She represents trust and unconditional hope that he can return to the light. Those hoping for a redemption for the son of Han and Leia share her optimistic request for him to join her. However, Ren rejects her entreaty and cements his path to the dark side.

▶ her quest into the dark sea cave to find out who she really is. What is remarkable is that the sequel trilogy's hero and villain, by way of their unique connection in the Force, create a strong impression of the duality that exists between the characters. Rey's the light, the hero, and Kylo's the dark, the hero's shadow. Rey represents hope, and Kylo its absence. Generally during the Hero's Journey, the hero is confronting these elements within themselves. In *The Last Jedi,* the Force itself becomes a character, with those two opposing sides facing the other. When Rey sits on the rocky outcrop with Luke asking her to look into the Force, she sees the light, the dark, the new life, and the destruction that exists within it. Perhaps it's the fact that Ren learns before Rey can admit to herself what she has always known—that she is the child of no notable bloodline (from his point of view)—that causes him to begin to doubt his own place in the galaxy. His lineage doesn't necessarily guarantee his position of greatness. He gains an understanding that his position must be earned.

This brings us to the Supreme Ordeal, which happens in Snoke's Throne Room after Rey has given herself up to the First Order in the hope of swaying Ren. The Ordeal requires the protagonist to pass a physical test or experience an emotional inner crisis while facing a deadly foe, drawing upon their lessons learned and skills acquired during the Tests. When Ren turns Rey's lightsaber toward Supreme Leader Snoke, then powers it up to cleave through him, he outwits his master—accomplishing something Darth Vader had not been able to in the two decades between *Revenge of the Sith* and *Return of the Jedi.* *The Last Jedi* relies heavily on the beats and visual cues of *Return of the Jedi* to drive home the closure Ren achieves as a villain. He finishes what his grandfather started—as he promises to do when addressing Vader's burnt helmet in *The Force Awakens*—and slays his master to seize control of the First

Order. This would be the Reward in the Vogler monomyth model.

For a Hero, this Reward is the means by which the character would help save their Ordinary World following the Road Back. While Rey struggles to find a way to save the last members of the Resistance, Kylo Ren marches the resources of the First Order toward their base on Crait, his intention to crush the Resistance and the mother he feels betrayed him. Earlier in the film, he fails a similar test to kill his mother when his finger hesitates on the trigger while flying his TIE silencer in the assault on the *Raddus.* By the end, he has resolved to address that error and intends to complete the task this time. (Though as a storytelling

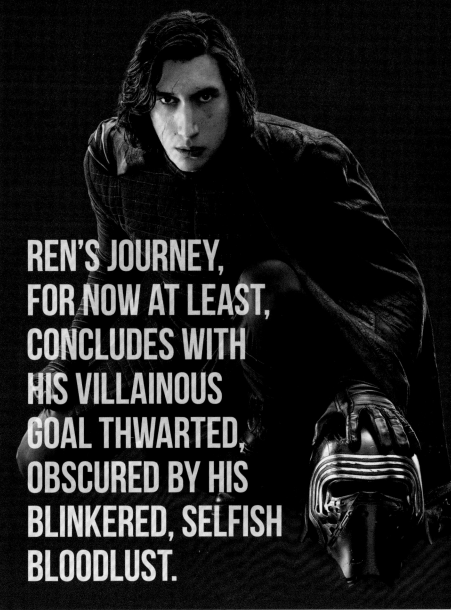

REN'S JOURNEY, FOR NOW AT LEAST, CONCLUDES WITH HIS VILLAINOUS GOAL THWARTED, OBSCURED BY HIS BLINKERED, SELFISH BLOODLUST.

point his earlier failure may have lulled some in the audience to believing Ren was drawing closer to deciding he was on the wrong path, rather than leading him to recommit to it.)

The Climax of Ren's Villain's Journey is the showdown with his former master. Rey, Ren's opposite, has convinced Luke there is hope. By leaving to confront Ren, she has also reminded Luke that being a Jedi requires selflessness. It is an incredibly selfless act to let go of the hate and anger Rey must feel, knowing what Ren did to Han Solo—a man who respected her enough to give her a chance at a better life and a man she knew to be a hero of the Rebellion. After a little more prodding from Yoda, Luke is

ready to let go of his guilt and fear of failure and try again. In the aftermath of Ren's battle with the Force-projection of Luke, one can imagine Luke sitting on Ahch-To reciting Yoda's mantra: Do or do not, there is no try.

From a distant rock, light years away, Luke fools Ren, who is intense and eager to finish the man responsible for Vader's 'failure' and who thought about killing him as an apprentice. As the First Order lets the might of its firepower rain down on the last Jedi, the deception might not have been apparent. But up close, in the personal confrontation, had Kylo Ren paid attention to his surroundings—the blue lightsaber

03 Ren and Rey share a deep connection through the Force, in *The Last Jedi.* (Left)

04 "You're no Vader. You're just a child in a mask," Snoke's chilling words to Kylo. (Left)

or the lack of footprints on the salt plain—he might have seen that Luke was using the same tactic as Poe in the opening scene, or Holdo during the second act, and using a diversion to buy the good guys more time, to find a way to survive. Ren's journey, for now at least, concludes with his villainous goal thwarted, obscured by his blinkered, selfish bloodlust. On the flipside of that moment, however, the remaining Resistance warriors are discovering that the light of the Jedi has returned to the galaxy, and that light's name is Rey. ☮

Tricia Barr is co-author of Ultimate Star Wars *and the* Star Wars Visual Encyclopedia. *Follow her on* **Twitter @fangirlcantina.**

A WALK ON THE DARK SIDE:

THE TALE OF ASAJJ VENTRESS

Sometimes a hero, sometimes a villain, Asajj Ventress is one of the most complex and fascinating characters in all of *Star Wars*...

WORDS: MEGAN CROUSE

Wicked laughter peals through the dark. The rustle of fabric, perhaps the hem of a skirt swishing along the ground—or is it just the wind? Then you're certain. Two red lightsabers flash through the shadows.

During the Clone Wars, Asajj Ventress struck fear into the hearts of her enemies. She also used terror to her advantage when she became a bounty hunter. A powerful Force user, she was nevertheless rejected by both the Jedi and the Sith.

Despite this, by the end of her life she had learned how to interact with people as something other than targets for her underworld missions. Ventress' life confirms what it says in the opening crawl for *Revenge of the Sith*. There are heroes on both sides of war.

Ventress wasn't introduced as a hero, however. As a major antagonist in both the *Clone Wars* micro-series and *The Clone Wars* television show, she clashed with Anakin Skywalker and Obi-Wan Kenobi thoughout the galaxy. While the Jedi had their own interpersonal dynamics—with Anakin getting used to training Ahsoka Tano as his Padawan and Ahsoka learning her own difficult lessons in wartime—personal struggles were also shaping

the actions of the Separatist leaders. Darth Sidious felt that Ventress was becoming powerful beyond just a mere assassin, and began threatening the balance maintained by the Sith "rule of two." To test Dooku's loyalty, Sidious demanded that he eliminate her, destroying what stability Ventress had and sending her on a journey to find allies who would not abandon her.

That series of abandonments continued in the novel *Dark Disciple*, in which Ventress and Quinlan Vos team up to fight Count Dooku, only for Quinlan to edge toward the dark side himself. Ventress' story is not just about the light side and the dark side, but the place in the middle.

"The Banshee"

As a fighter, Ventress cultivates a frightening persona. She uses two lightsabers in an acrobatic and ferocious fighting style. As well as being proficient enough with the lightsabers to hold her own against Anakin and Obi-Wan, she is also powerful in the Force, able to choke both Jedi at once, and apt to end fights with a brutal display of Force power. In hand-to-hand combat she uses body blows and throws, taking advantage of her long limbs and luring the enemy close to her center of gravity. She also uses the Force to subtly speed up her attacks and predict where an opponent's next move might come from. She is

01

02

deadly even without her lightsabers.

Ventress is also a driven and focused warrior. When working as a bounty hunter, she forcefully tells her Jedi partner Quinlan Vos that she won't permit any "foolish errors. No lost quarries because you want to make a grand gesture. I won't tolerate laziness or stupidity."

She named her starship the *Banshee* after people referred to her by that monster's name for her triumphant laughter and raspy voice. In the real world, the banshee is a creature from Irish mythology. Her screams are said to foretell the death of a family member. That association is particularly appropriate for Ventress, since she has lost almost everyone who cared about her in a life filled with pain.

The first loss, and the one that set her on her dark path, is the loss of her true parents. Ventress' mother belongs to the Nightsister clan, the society of Force-using witches led by Mother Talzin. Ventress is given up as part of a deal made with a Siniteen slaver named Hal'sted.

When Hal'sted is shot and killed by Weequay pirates, however, Jedi Master Ky Narec finds the young Dathomirian alone. He takes her under his wing and, for a time, the pair defend the people of the planet Rattatak from pirates and warlords. When Ky Narec is killed, however, dying in Ventress' arms, she embraces the dark side as a balm for her loss and presents herself to Count Dooku as a potential apprentice.

Ventress does not find the security and triumph she desires by working with Dooku, either. Their relationship is a twisted version of the loyalty shown between Jedi Masters and apprentices, but it does allow

Ventress some stability and a sense of purpose, something she always needs. She feels that he appreciates her, and that seems at least partly true. When Sidious tells Dooku to kill Ventress, he hesitates—before agreeing to have Ventress assassinated.

"Nothing There but Fog and Witches"

One of Ventress' greatest strengths is her ability to survive no matter the odds. Dooku thinks that he can control her story, but he cannot. She survives the assassination attempt and returns to the one place she thought she might find a

"IT TAKES VENTRESS IDENTIFYING WITH OTHER PEOPLE FOR HER TO TURN AWAY FROM HER VISCIOUS PHILOSOPHY."

future, Dathomir, her homeworld. Though she is still steeped in dark side magic as she attempts to get revenge on Dooku, Dathomir is the first place she has visited in a long time where she feels she is among family. Mother Talzin nurses her wounds and offers her a place to stay among the Nightsisters. Ventress even finds companions, the warriors Karis and Naa'leth.

Unfortunately, another one of Ventress' most important relationships at this time mirrors exactly what caused Ventress so much suffering in the first place. She essentially enslaves Savage Opress, training him ruthlessly as Dooku trained her. She even oversees while Savage kills his own brother, forcing someone else to experience the same pain she experienced when she lost the Jedi Master with whom she was so close. Throughout her life, Ventress adheres to the Sith belief that in order to gain power, one must

be willing to kill anything or anyone who stands in the way.

The Nightsisters themselves are cruel, and Ventress feels right at home with them. Karis says that she is honored to consider Ventress her sister. Mother Talzin also encourages Ventress to side with the Nightsisters against Count Dooku, and seems to reassure her when she says: "You have your breath, your skill, and your sisters. Everything you need to survive."

It might indeed be reassuring for Ventress to know that these things can guarantee her survival. But Talzin is also trying to use Ventress for her own ends in the same way Dooku did. Reassuring Ventress that no one except the Nightsisters will support her is just another way to bring her more firmly under their control. Ventress likes this warlike family, but it also shows one of the fundamental themes of *Star Wars*: that the dark side corrupts its users, seducing them with power and comfort before leading them to misery and destruction. This is the case when Dooku sends Grievous to get revenge against the Nightsisters.

Grievous' forces massacre Ventress' people, leaving her adrift once again and saddened that she doesn't know how to perform any of the funeral rites that gave the Nightsisters the power to raise undead soldiers.

It takes Ventress identifying with other people for her to turn away from her vicious philosophy. Two people in particular help her begin to turn toward the light: Pluma Sodi and Obi-Wan Kenobi.

Finding a Home
Late in the Clone Wars, Jedi Council member Mace Windu says that Ventress has "failed at being the perfect Sith." He points out that she has tried to kill Dooku several times without success.

She does succeed at making a precarious living as a bounty hunter, living on Tatooine and on Coruscant's infamous Level 1313. While there she joins a group of bounty hunters under ▶

01 Asajj was a hero, a villain, and a smuggler in her storied life (left).

02 Jedi training helped make Ventress lethal with a lightsaber (left).

the command of a young Boba Fett, but they aren't what she's looking for in a new family, and she has no respect for the still inexperienced Boba. It is during one of these jobs that she meets Pluma Sodi, a girl that the bounty hunters were assigned to escort.

Pluma was kidnapped from her family by the corrupt Belugan dictator, Otua Blank, who wanted to make the girl into his bride. At first, Ventress has no emotional stake in the fight. Interested only in the money she could get at the end of the job, she finds the girl's plight distasteful, but still doesn't understand the appeal of doing good for its own sake. She was too young to internalize her Jedi Master's compassion, and subsequent teaching from Dooku and Talzin, who are both more than willing to manipulate other people's lives to serve their own ends, had only overwritten her natural capacity for kindness.

Pluma tries her best to appeal to Ventress. "I never asked to be ripped away from my home, from my family. You'll never know what it's like," she says. While Ventress doesn't change her mind, it does make her think about how their situations are so similar.

However, Boba gives her an

opportunity to change her mind. When he refuses to share the bounty, Ventress stuffs him in the girl's cage and lets Pluma go free instead. Ventress' smug expression afterward shows her glorying in her own ability to control the situation. She also distributes the bounty evenly among all the hunters, even Boba, showing her own sort of honor.

With the money from the job in her pocket and Pluma (and Boba) both safely freed, Ventress realizes that she now has the freedom to do whatever she wants. There are still some loose ends that she needs to tie up, however—ends that will lead her right to the Jedi.

Ventress always had an affinity to Obi-Wan, bantering with him as well as battling. The pair become unlikely allies when Ventress sneaks onto Savage Opress' ship in an effort to tie up that particular loose end. She finds Darth Maul, who forces her into an alliance with Obi-Wan in a four-way lightsaber fight. As well as showing off Ventress' impressive martial skills and how her intimidation tactics work on even the Sith Lord, she also shows some trust in Obi-Wan. She lets him use one of her lightsabers, but assures

"VENTRESS HAD AN AFFINITY FOR OBI-WAN, BANTERING WITH HIM AS WELL AS FIGHTING."

him that one fight doesn't make them allies. When Obi-Wan asks, "When did you become the good guy?" Ventress responds with "Don't insult me." Ventress helps Obi-Wan escape, but it will take a couple more encounters with Jedi for her to reach the light.

Deals With The Jedi
The Ventress of level 1313 is a driven woman without a purpose in life. Her bounty hunting jobs, while prestigious enough for her to keep her fearsome reputation, do not pay enough money for her to leave Coruscant's dangerous lower levels. She clings to the idea of her own determination.

Her next bounty brings her to an encounter with Ahsoka Tano, while the Padawan is on the run. Ventress is still driven primarily by money and a need for revenge, but Ahsoka offers her a pardon

03 Asajj comes saber-to-saber with Anakin.

04 Ventress' skills were a match for any opponent (right).

05 Despite her prowess, Ventress is not invincible (right).

and a chance to fight a person who might be Dooku's new apprentice. Ventress again is not swayed by the philosophy of the Jedi, and makes sure Ahsoka knows that her help is not guaranteed.

However, it's a conversation after Ahsoka has returned to the temple that really reveals the emotion that has been stewing beneath Ventress' surly surface. She tells Anakin: "I realized that your fallen Padawan and I had a lot in common... my Master abandoned me and that's exactly what you did to her. You and your precious Jedi Order."

Ventress identifies with Ahsoka now that she is on the run and cut off from her adopted family. Looking ahead, we can also see that this might also be a pivotal moment for Anakin. When Darth Sidious begins to plant doubt about

the Jedi Council in Anakin's mind in *Revenge of the Sith*, he may well think back to this moment and remember Ventress' words to him and how the Council put Ahsoka on trial.

Ventress' last defining personal relationship is with a very different Jedi: Quinlan Vos, with whom she develops a romantic relationship.

Her relationship with Vos is one of her first in which there is no power struggle. Unlike her time with Savage, Ventress does not see Vos as an attack dog whom she can send out on missions as she pleases. They work together, and she begins to experience what it's like to have an easy, equal partnership with another person.

Their partnership taking a romantic turn is also a new experience for her. While she

has used her physical wiles as a way to entrap her victims before, she has never been in a true, equal partnership with someone before. This change brings her both joy and tragedy. In the end, she elects to sacrifice her life for Vos and, of the two of them, she is the one who argues that the path to the dark side only leads to suffering.

"Nothing is ever enough," she tells Vos. "You get more, and more, but you're never happy. It's a trap baited with all the things you want most in life—and it's not worth living. I already left that behind."

She sees that her quest to find a family led her down a dark path with the Nightsisters, and that her existence as a bounty hunter afterward was merely one job after another, without any friends or family to support or enrich her.

This change of heart and new-found wisdom comes about not only because of Vos, but also because of her encounters with the other Jedi and her personal search for meaning. The decision to sacrifice herself is hers alone and—similar to Luke Skywalker's willingness to lay down his lightsaber instead of fighting Darth Vader— it shows that she has developed an inner strength. In Ventress' case, however, she does not get to live to see her new future.

04

She is gifted one final vision, in which she sees that "burning vengeance that only increased the hunger for more" is not the only path open to her. She tells Vos to return to the Jedi, then joins her sisters in death, finally recovering the family that she once lost.

Ventress was a Jedi, a would-be Sith, and a bounty hunter—almost everything except a quiet citizen. She survived enough loss and pain for four lifetimes, becoming in the process both a memorable hero and a complex villain. ☻

05

THE MAKING OF
MAUL

Marvel Comics' *Darth Maul* is a five-part miniseries that sheds light on the sinister Force-wielder's early days. Here, writer Cullen Bunn tells us about scripting the Zabrak's backstory—and falling for his double-bladed charms!

WORDS: MICHAEL KOGGE

If you thought Darth Maul's death at the hands of Obi-Wan Kenobi (again... this time in *Star Wars: Rebels*) was the last we'd be seeing of the sinister Force-wielder, you were mistaken. Set prior to Maul's first appearance in *The Phantom Menace*, Marvel's new mini-series proves there are many more Maul stories to tell, as writer Cullen Bunn tells *Star Wars Insider*.

Star Wars Insider: How did you get the job writing *Darth Maul*?
Cullen Bunn: I was at the Marvel offices in 2015, a few months after the current *Star Wars* comic launched, and I cornered [editor] Jordan D. White, saying I'd love to try a *Star Wars* title! At the time, there were several books already in the works, so I had to be patient. But a little over a year ago, Jordan called and asked if I'd be interested in doing a Darth Maul book.

I was thrilled. *Star Wars* has been a huge influence for me. I vividly remember getting my first few action figures, and I can still recall sitting down in the theater to watch the first movie. I had *Star Wars* wallpaper and bed sheets. I hoarded the action figures. I sent away for Kenner's mail-in Boba Fett figure. My parents took me out of school to see *Return of the Jedi*! I was a fanatic. It's an amazing feeling to be contributing to that universe after all these years.

What is *Darth Maul* all about?
It starts with Maul chafing under the edicts of Darth Sidious, in the days before *The Phantom Menace*. Sidious has trained him to hate the Jedi, but now he won't let him strike. To vent his frustration, he is pitting himself against some of the nastiest prey in the galaxy—rathtars

in the first issue, for example—but it's not enough. When he finds out there's a Jedi Padawan being held prisoner by a nefarious crime lord, he decides to sneak away and kill the Padawan before his master knows he's gone. It's a risky play, because he has to keep his Sith identity a secret from the Jedi—and if Sidious finds out what he's up to, the punishment will be severe!

Are the Padawan and the crime lord new characters? What can you tell us about them?
The Padawan is Eldra Kaitis. I've only been writing her for a short time, but she's already one of my favorite characters. She's a skilled Padawan, and Maul sees that she must be on the fast track to being a Jedi Knight. She's eager and

plucky, and she takes no guff–not even from the likes of Darth Maul! When she first lays eyes on him, she doesn't react with fear. Her reaction is to ask, "Who are you supposed to be?"

If Maul wants to kill her—and he does—he's going to have a fight on his hands!

The crime lord is Xev Xrexus. She is unlike most of the underworld bosses we've seen in *Star Wars*. She's charming and pleasant, and throws lavish events where she's a friendly host. Sure, she's willing to assassinate anyone who gets in her way, but her parties are awesome! She's right out in the open, and that's unusual for Maul, who has worked in the shadows for so long.

How did *The Phantom Menace* influence your approach to the story?
There's a famous moment in *The Phantom Menace* where Maul is battling Qui-Gon and they get separated by a force-field wall. Qui-Gon takes a meditative stance, but

**PROFILE
CULLEN BUNN**
Cullen made his name with horror series *The Damned* for Oni Press in 2008. He went on to create *The Sixth Gun* and *The Tooth* for Oni, and to write for the likes of *Deadpool* and *Uncanny X-Men* at Marvel, and *Aquaman* and *Green Lantern* at DC. His prose work includes the children's novel *Crooked Hills* and short story collection *Creeping Stones & Other Stories*. Raised in rural North Carolina, he now lives in Missouri, with his wife and son.

01 Maul on the hunt, in "Darth Maul" Issue 1. Art by Luke Ross.

02 A pack of rathtars are no match for a Sith Lord. Art by Luke Ross.

01

02

Maul paces back and forth impatiently, seething. That small moment influenced me more than anything else in the movie, and I wanted to make sure we channeled that rage and impatience.

Maul's most recent appearances have been in *Star Wars Rebels*. Will fans of that version recognize this character?
Oh, yeah. The two incarnations are more similar than you might think. We only see Maul for a few minutes in *The Phantom Menace*. Comparatively, *The Clone Wars* and *Rebels* really dig into the character. On television, he

> **"My parents took me out of school to see *Return of the Jedi*! I was a fanatic."**

obviously gets a little more time to shine, and we see him as cunning and cruel, not just a rage-filled weapon. In the comic, I wanted to explore how he's always had those characteristics, but has also always struggled with his hunger for vengeance.

With Maul as the main character, is there a risk of making him too sympathetic?
I've written a lot of villainous characters over the years, and striking the right balance is extremely important. It helps that for a good portion of the series, he is dealing with enemies who are just as bad as he is. But I'm definitely not trying to make Maul into the good guy. I just want readers to understand why he feels the way he does, even if it is impossible to agree with him. I've tried to give an insight to the ideology that's been pounded into Maul's head: the

Jedi are evil; they murdered the Sith because the Sith wanted freedom from their order; the Jedi must be punished. In a lot of ways, Maul is a tragic character, but he's not a hero.

Will we learn more about the master-apprentice relationship between Sidious and Maul? Do they respect each other? Maybe even fear each other?
The relationship between master and apprentice is very important in this book. And you're right about fear, which is a big part of the dark side. I think Sidious is wary of Maul's violent, rage-filled nature, even though he helped develop it. He isn't afraid Maul might cut loose on him, though: he fears what Maul's rage could do to his plans. Sidious is a master planner and manipulator. He needs everything set up in just the right way. That's why he keeps Maul on such a short leash. ▶

04

Has writing for Maul changed how you think about him?
Yes, in that I never expected him to be so charming! I knew I would have the chance to explore some of his more sympathetic qualities, but I didn't expect him to be a charismatic person. I think that's one of the most surprising things that come across in this book.

What's your process for writing an issue?
First I do a rough outline to figure out the major "beats" of each issue, and those are usually just handwritten in a notebook. Then, I do a detailed beat-by-beat outline, listing all the panels on each page. That can be used to create the entire comic, except for dialogue. I send the outline to my editors, who send it to the good folks at Lucasfilm for approval. Once the outline is approved, I write a full script. That's not just dialogue: it's also description to give the artist a good sense of what's going on with each page, and the mood of the story as a whole.

What's it like working with artist Luke Ross?
Luke is a wonderful collaborator. He usually sends pages in batches, so I have to wait a bit, and then 10 pages show up in my inbox and I'm blown away. He's a master at getting the likenesses and expressions of these characters onto the page. He brings a grittiness that I think we need for this story. And his action sequences, with Maul leaping and spinning and kicking, are awesome.

03 "*Darth Maul*" Issue 1 variant cover art by Mark Brooks.

04 A rathtar takes a lunch break. Art by Luke Ross.

What are your favorite moments from the *Maul* series?
Tough question! There's a flashback to Maul's days in training where Sidious takes Maul to Malachor. That's a really creepy scene that helps set up some of what's to come for Maul. I love that we've been able to connect the dots like that and touch on wider *Star Wars* lore.

I also really enjoy the interactions Maul has with Cad Bane and Aurra Sing, who are two of my favorite bounty hunters. They have a huge role in the series and bring an "outside looking in" perspective on what Maul is up to.

Any scene with both Maul and Eldra is a lot of fun to write, too. They're always having one conversation on the surface and another on a much deeper level. They aren't friends by any stretch of the imagination, but there is a kind of kinship between them that I like.

"The relationship between master and apprentice is very important in this book."

How do you explain the enduring appeal of Darth Maul, who was only on the big screen for such a short time?
I think he's so popular *because* he only had a short time on the big screen. For me, he was the coolest thing in *The Phantom Menace*. He was dark and menacing and scary. When he fires up that double-lightsaber and "Duel of the Fates" begins to play, I get chills. But we didn't get enough. He was the Boba Fett of the prequel trilogy. He's an incredibly cool addition to the mythos and we know he has more of a story, so we want to see it! ☻

LEGENDARY STORIES:
TALES OF THE SITH

MICHAEL KOGGE TAKES A LOOK BACK ON THE FINAL ISSUES OF TALES OF THE JEDI,
AS THE SITH TOOK CENTER STAGE!

"My Lord, it's impossible to locate the ship. It's out of our range." "Not for a Sith."

A s hard as it might be to believe, this exchange between Nute Gunray and Darth Sidious in *The Phantom Menace* marked the first time the word "Sith" was spoken in a *Star Wars* film. Yet in the twenty-two years before Episode I's release in 1999, even casual film fans had learned that the Jedi's legendary enemies were called the Sith. It's a testament to the power of *Star Wars*' spin-off merchandise such as books, games, and comics that few were surprised when Sidious revealed the name of the Jedi nemeses on-screen two decades later.

In fact, the Sith had been part of the *Star Wars* mythology since its inception. While writing the early drafts of the screenplay, George Lucas found inspiration in many science fiction authors, among them Edgar Rice Burroughs, who used "Sith" in his 1913 serialized novel *Warlord of Mars* as a name for giant alien hornets. Lucas played around with the word, first calling his villains the "Black Knights of Sith" before settling on "Dark Lord of the Sith" to identify Darth Vader in his second draft:

The awesome, seven-foot-tall BLACK KNIGHT OF THE SITH makes his way into the blinding light of the cockpit area. This is LORD DARTH VADER, right hand to the MASTER OF THE SITH.

True to their secretive nature, the Sith didn't need to be acknowledged in movie dialogue to trickle down from Lucas's screenplay into the variety of ancillary merchandise, like the Marvel Comics adaptation and the Del Rey novelization. Over the years, just as fans clamored to know more about the Jedi Knights, they wondered the same about these mysterious Sith. Some even went to the lengths of producing their own stories, such as Nicole Courtney's radio play *The Dark Lords of the Sith*, which won the grand prize for *Bantha Tracks*' 1983 Creativity Contest.

In the early 1990s, when Dark Horse Comics acquired the *Star Wars* license, Lucasfilm permitted more about the Jedi and Sith of yore to be divulged. Writer Tom Veitch, fresh off his success with the *Dark Empire* comic, set his new series, Tales of the Jedi, four thousand years before *A New Hope*. In this era, Veitch established that the Jedi Knights of the Old Republic believed they had wiped out all the Sith, yet remnants of Sith alchemy lay in museums and the evil spirit of the Sith Lord Freedon Nadd haunted the tombs of the planet Onderon. Veitch's approach unveiled bits and pieces about the Sith issue by issue, giving the Jedi a strong antagonist, yet allowing most of the Sith history to remain mysterious.

DARK LORD OR DARK LORDS?

The original Tales of the Jedi five-issue series and two-parter, *The Freedon Nadd Uprising*, sold so well that Veitch was able to explore more about the Jedi's war against the Sith darksiders. For the next installment set in the Tales era, he teamed up with *Star Wars* novelist Kevin J. Anderson. "I got to know Tom Veitch because I started reading the Dark Empire books and I wanted to include those events in my Jedi Academy trilogy," Anderson says. "I had the spirit of a long dead Dark Lord of the Sith who happened to live thousands of years before the films. The light bulb went on over both of our heads at the same time and we said, 'Well, what if your Dark Lord of the Sith guy happened to be living at the same time as my Jedi guys were?' We decided to pool our skills and ended up telling that full-blown story of the Dark Lords of the Sith and the Sith War, which was the whole origin story of Exar Kun and Ulic Qel-Droma."

Together, Veitch and Anderson made their bold proposal to tell these "tales of the Sith." Lucasfilm was understandably hesitant. At this time, the first prequel film was only in its initial stages and no one knew what, if anything, George Lucas might do with the Sith. He had not yet established the "Rule of Two," the idea there could be only one Sith Lord and one apprentice at a time. "They said, 'George will never go for this,'" Veitch recalls. "Fortunately for all of us, he loved the idea."

> GOSSETT DESIGNED WHAT WOULD BECOME AN ICONIC WEAPON IN THE PREQUEL TRILOGY.

TWIN BLADES

Upon Lucasfilm's approval, Veitch traveled to Anderson's house in Colorado and hammered out ideas during sessions that lasted five or six hours. Their collaboration resulted in the best-selling series Dark Lords of the Sith, with the first five issues penciled by Chris Gossett and the last by Art Wetherell.

During the concept stage, Gossett designed what would become an iconic weapon in the prequel trilogy: the double-bladed lightsaber. Gossett had started messing around with lightsabers in the original Tales of the Jedi series. "The ancient Jedi would not have all made flashlight length handles for their weapons. They would have experimented," he says. "I proposed that lightsabers in the Old Republic look more handcrafted, like weapons from feudal Japan." A prime example of this was the lightsaber Gossett supplied Twi'lek Jedi Tott Doneeta. Its curved hilt resembled a Japanese katana.

However, it would be the double-bladed lightsaber Gossett envisioned for dark Jedi Exar Kun that would capture fans' imaginations. Though Kun did not use it until *The Sith War*, which was drawn by Dario Carrasco, it was Gossett who conceived of this ideal Sith weapon. Such a unique design caused nervousness at Lucasfilm, as it truly pushed what was seen in the films. But after some creative back-and-forth with Dark Horse editor Dan Thorsland, they approved Gossett's design. Five years later, Gossett was overjoyed to see Darth Maul wield the dual blades in *The Phantom Menace*.

"THESE LIGHTSABERS BELONG TO THE JEDI..."

"...I WILL PROTECT THEM WITH MY LIFE, IF I MUST!"

"A PITY... LOOKS LIKE I'LL BE CHOPPING WOOD TODAY!"

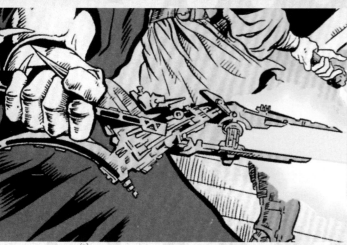

PERHAPS THE AGE COULD SHIFT THE TONES OF GREEN, BROWN, ETC. YOUNGER TREE DWELLERS COULD BE A BRIGHT "TREE FROG" TYPE OF GREEN — WITH THE ELDERS TAKING ON A MORE BROWN COLOR. AT ANY RATE, I LIKE GREENS AND BROWNS TOGETHER FOR THEM. KIND OF A CAMOUFLAGE YOU KNOW, NATURE. IT DOES THAT.

Opposite page, from top: Design sketches by Carrasco for Aarrba the Hutt; Jori Pathfinder (later Daragon) in the *Golden Age of the Sith*; the first double-bladed lightsaber, as wielded by the Dark Jedi Exar Kun. Chris Gossett originated this idea in an unused concept sketch for *Dark Lords of the Sith*, which Dario Carrasco later drew upon for his depiction of Exar Kun in the pages of *The Sith War*.

This page, clockwise from top: Exar Kun reveals his double-bladed lightsaber in a panel from *The Sith War* pencilled by Dario Carrasco, Jr.; one of Gossett's unique handgrip designs for the ancient Jedi; Gossett's 1993 concept sketch for Master Ood Bnar; a 2012 sketch of Mandalore by Dario Carrasco.

NEW TEAM, NEW TALES

*D*ark Lords was a resounding success, and Dark Horse immediately commissioned a sequel series, *The Sith War*. Veitch and Anderson co-plotted the first two issues, then Anderson took the reins while Veitch stepped away. Those two issues would be Veitch's final contribution to the *Star Wars* universe after many years of stories.

A new artist also entered the fold. Thirty-three year-old Dario Carrasco, Jr., had received his degree in architecture from the Technological University of the Philippines in Manila and spent a few years as a draftsman in Saudi Arabia. But his dream since elementary school in the Philippines was to become a comic book artist. He immigrated to Canada to pursue his passion and, as soon as he landed in Vancouver, he sent samples out to Marvel Comics. It wasn't until he met the editors at the San Diego Comic-Con that his samples were passed along, and he landed his first assignment to pencil *Alpha Flight* from issue #125. He continued to work on Marvel titles, penciling the Pinhead mini-series in the Epic line, until the company went bankrupt in 1994.

This sad turn of events had a happy ending that led Carrasco into the galaxy far, far away. "On one particular Sunday, I was a guest in a local convention in Vancouver," Carrasco remembers. "I met an old acquaintance and a special guest, Diana Schutz, who was also the editor-in-chief at Dark Horse at the time. When she saw me, she asked if I was doing any work and I mentioned to her about the lay-off at Marvel. She asked for some samples that she could bring back to Dark Horse with her. The following week she put me in contact with [editor] Bob Cooper who asked me to do a one-page sample. The rest is history."

Drawing *Star Wars* professionally was a dream come true. Carrasco had been a fan of the saga as a teenager growing up in the Philippines. "I saw the first sequel [*The Empire Strikes Back*] when I was in high school. It got imprinted in my mind so much that when I stepped into university, I sketched my own sci-fi universe in my notebook, complete with ships, creatures, and main characters. One of my classmates and a very good fan of my work and a friend, asked me to give him the notebook. I signed it and I gave it to him."

TALES OF THE TALES

When Carrasco met the tight deadline and finished off The Sith War, Bob Cooper asked him to draw the next two Tales series, which would also be scripted by Kevin J. Anderson. Instead of being a sequel, they would be prequels, set a thousand years in the past, with the evocative titles: *Golden Age of the Sith* and *Fall of the Sith Empire*. On these series, Carrasco didn't have to emulate Gossett's style. He could flex his own creative muscle designing new characters, spaceships, and aliens.

"I'm a history buff myself and the early history of *Star Wars* was my cup of tea," Carrasco says. "Both of my ideas of design for *Golden Age* and *Fall* were taken from the influences of feudal Japan mixed with Mesopotamian and Egyptian backgrounds."

Lucasfilm's only restriction was that Carrasco and Anderson make no direct copy of a human historical setting, because *Star Wars* was a separate universe unto itself. "If an influence taken from our history could be improved upon, as long as the design was alien in structure, it was good with Lucasfilm," Carrasco says.

Carrasco also put his architectural experience to good use throughout the series, particularly in one essential *Star Wars* moment. "I have a lot of favorite scenes, but my most memorable was the epic battle in the city of Coruscant in *Fall*. The wide spreads were very intricate and detailed. I had such fun doing them. It's like I'm looking into the lens of that unforgettable event in Tales of the Jedi. If I had to do Tales again, I wouldn't do it any other way. I was so proud of the work I put in these series."

THE FINAL TALE OF A JEDI

After *Golden Age* and *Fall*, Dark Horse commissioned Anderson to write and Gossett to pencil *Redemption*, a five-issue finale to the Tales series that would complete the story of Ulic Qel-Droma. Although Veitch had written a long treatment outlining Qel-Droma's ultimate fate, Anderson and Gossett decided to take the conclusion in another direction. Gossett stayed at Anderson's house for a week where they beat out the story, page-by-page, panel-by-panel.

"I told him I wanted to work closely with him on the layouts to keep the panel count low and that if we were going to [SPOILER ALERT!] go so far as to kill Ulic Qel Droma, then I really wanted to collaborate with him on how we did so," Gossett says. "He was very open to it and very accepting of ideas."

Redemption was not only a profound emotional experience for its protagonist, but also its creators.

"It was very powerful for us because we lived with this guy for so long and he was so close to us," Anderson says. "I remember just plotting out these last pages and how Ulic came to his end —a kind of heroic, but surprising end—and Chris is sitting across the table and he's sketching these last panels and he looked up at me, and he just had tears pouring down his face. He was just so moved by what we were doing. That's the best moment of the entire comic writing experience, I got to tell you."

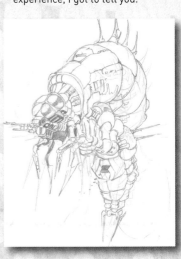

REDEMPTION WAS A PROFOUND EMOTIONAL EXPERIENCE FOR ITS CREATORS.

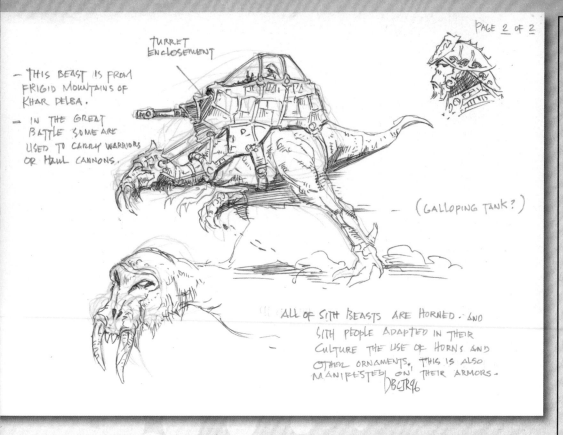

TURRET ENCLOSEMENT

PAGE 2 OF 2

- THIS BEAST IS FROM FRIGID MOUNTAINS OF KHAR DELBA.

- IN THE GREAT BATTLE SOME ARE USED TO CARRY WARRIORS OR HAUL CANNONS.

(GALLOPING TANK?)

ALL OF SITH BEASTS ARE HORNED. AND SITH PEOPLE ADAPTED IN THEIR CULTURE THE USE OF HORNS AND OTHER ORNAMENTS. THIS IS ALSO MANIFESTED ON THEIR ARMORS.
DBCTR96

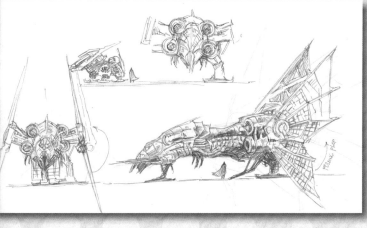

MANUAL FLAP

DARIO,

LUCASFILM LIKED ALL YOUR NEW SKETCHES EXCEPT FOR THE "DARK LORD SARCOPHAGUS — WHICH THEY SAY LOOKS A LITTLE BIT TOO MUCH LIKE AN EGYPTIAN SARCOPHAGUS. THEY'D LIKE YOU TO REVISE THIS ONE DESIGN & RESUBMIT IT.
BOB

NEW LORD SARCOPHAGUS

FUNERAL PROCESSION OF DARK LORDS

Opposite page, clockwise from top: Another Carrasco concept sketch for Mandalore, stating he's at least 7' tall; a Mandalore "bug" ship designed by Carrasco; surface of the Sith planet Korriban, inspired by Carrasco's fascination with Egyptian and Mesopotamian history.

This page, from top: Carrasco's designs for the "Sith beasts" that Sith warriors would mount and ride; concept sketches for Exar Kun's warship by Carrasco; Bob Cooper writes to Carrasco: "Lucasfilm liked all your new sketches except for the Dark Lord sarcophagus— which they say looks too much like an Egyptian sarcophagus. They'd like you to revise the one design and resubmit it."

FUTURE TALES

After 35 issues over five years, revealing much of the history of the legendary Jedi and the Sith, Tales of the Jedi officially came to an end with *Redemption*. But that proved just the beginning for this era of *Star Wars*. The computer game Knights of the Old Republic relied on the comic series as source material to build a virtual Old Republic, and the game, in turn, spawned a comic series set 40 years after Tales, which ran for 50 issues. Moreover, the Expanded Universe novels (now Legends) and even the *Star Wars: The Clone Wars* television show drew inspiration from the Jedi and Sith lore that Veitch and Anderson had developed.

While it's been over 20 years since Tales of the Jedi began, the series remains a special memory for its creator and instigator, Tom Veitch. "I'm happy to have had the chance to work on the comics, and I confess that sometimes when my wife and I are talking about *Star Wars*, the ideas and images will start to flow. It's a galaxy of infinite possibilities." ✦

LOST IN TRANSLATION?

DARTH VADER'S ITALIAN VOICE ACTOR, MASSIMO FOSCHI, SHARES SOME MEMORIES OF BRINGING INTERGALACTIC MALEVOLENCE TO ROME...
WORDS: CALUM WADDELL

"Se solo tu conoscessi il potere del lato oscuro!"

Massimo Foschi: The voice of Darth Vader in Italy! Photo by Calum Waddell

Actor Massimo Foschi might be best known to fans of Italian cult cinema for his starring role in the gut-crunching classic *Last Cannibal World* (1977). Directed by Ruggero Deodato, who later made the more notorious *Cannibal Holocaust* (1980), the film was a surprise success and launched an entire genre of jungle-based meat-munching movies. However, Foschi is also a respected voice work veteran in his home country—with his most famous work being on the original *Star Wars* trilogy.

Beginning with *A New Hope* in 1977, Foschi was brought in to loop the menacing Darth Vader into Italian so that native-speaking audiences in areas such as Milan, Rome, and Venice could also enjoy the space fantasy epic...

"*Star Wars* totally changed my life," begins the actor, speaking exclusively to *Star Wars Insider*. "Even today, people around Rome recognize me. To the Italian audience, I was 'Darth Vader' in each of these three movies. I have children and adults come up to me on the street today and say, 'Please will you repeat my favorite lines?' The most common request is 'No, Luke... I am your father' from *The Empire Strikes Back*. Although I have also been asked to say 'May the Force be with you' which, of course, is not even a Darth Vader line!"

"EVEN TODAY, PEOPLE AROUND ROME RECOGNIZE ME. TO THE ITALIAN AUDIENCE, I WAS DARTH VADER!"

A classically trained actor, Foschi is also something of a genre veteran. He dubbed for Lance Henriksen in *Aliens* (1986) and most recently added some continental mannerisms to Donald Sutherland in the Hunger Games series. He also returned to *Star Wars* in 2005 for the climactic prequel *Revenge of the Sith*, wherein he once again gave an Italian voice to Darth Vader.

"That was a lot of fun," he admits, before revealing that he felt no pressure about putting his own aural twist on the iconic villain. "Of course, Darth Vader was James Earl Jones, but that was fine for me. My job was to make the character distinct for local people—so although I was inspired by his talents, I felt as if I could still bring something a little different. He certainly has a great voice though!"

Indeed, for Foschi, it is the ability to put his own interpretation onto an established English-language role that bagged him the *Star Wars* job. "I had been dubbing a number of big Hollywood actors before I got *Star Wars*," he adds. "I was already recognized in Italy for voicing such greats as Laurence Olivier, Kirk Douglas, Gregory Peck, Charles Dance and many other tremendous performers. That was how I got called in and asked if I might want to take on the challenge of dubbing James Earl Jones. Of course, I said 'yes.' I loved science fiction films and I could tell that this was going to be one of the best."

Asked about his final thoughts on his time verbalizing George Lucas's most celebrated antagonist, Foschi is quick to paraphrase a line from the famous space opera...

"All I can say to each and every person who continues to love and celebrate these films is 'May the Force remain strong with you,'" he laughs. "Such fan enthusiasm keeps this type of cinema alive for many generations to come." ☻

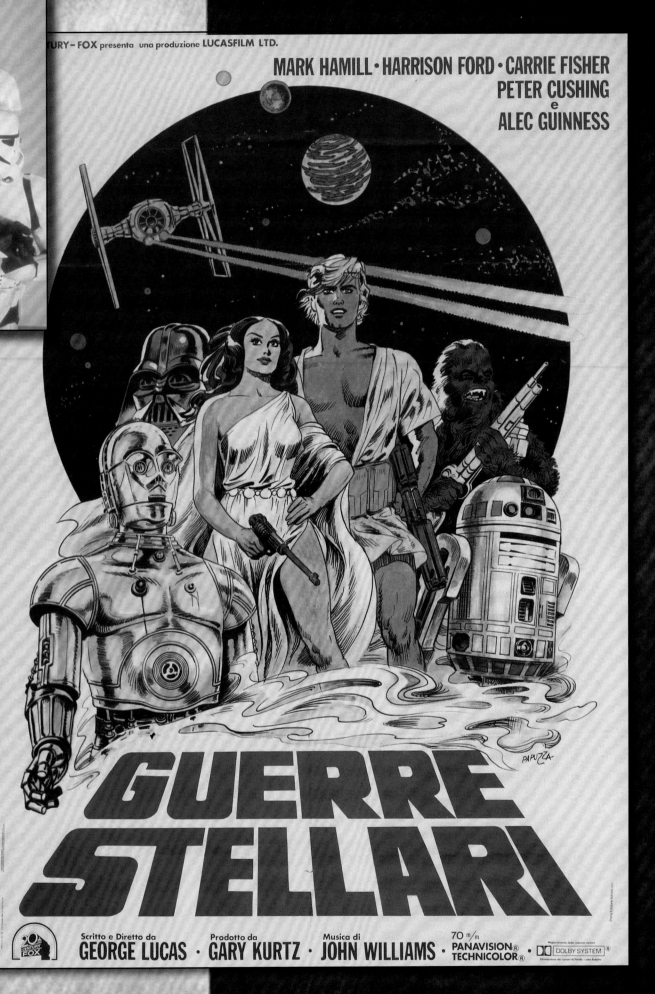

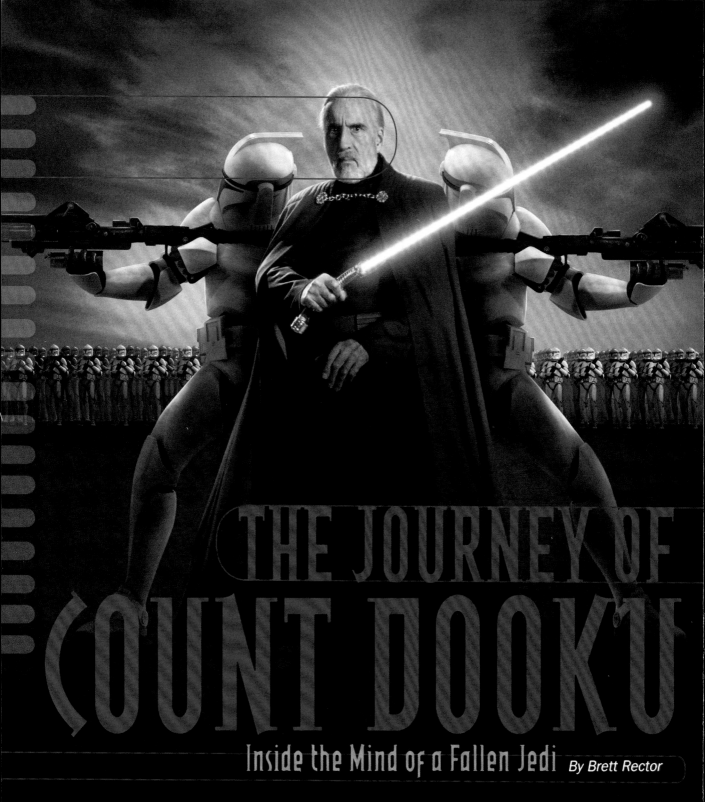

THE JOURNEY OF COUNT DOOKU

Inside the Mind of a Fallen Jedi

By Brett Rector

He is the actor of a thousand faces, and his illustrious career is well into its eighth decade. He has worked with some of the world's most well-known actors, and he has shared the stage with hundreds more. He may have gone toe to toe with Errol Flynn, but he will be most remembered for his epic confrontation with Yoda. He perfected the art of playing the villain, yet his demeanor is anything but villainous. He is, by all

hristopher Lee will go down in cinematic history as one of the most prolific actors that ever lived. However, now is not the time to wax philosophical about the man who breathed life into Count Dracula but rather to delve into the mind of the man who portrays Count Dooku. Recently, the soft-spoken actor gave his views on George Lucas, the story at large, and the corruption of the Jedi.

Now that you've played the character in two movies what do you find fascinating about Count Dooku?

For one, his name, which means "poison" in Japanese. Something I'm sure George probably knew. It's a very appropriate name because he's very lethal. The character himself is fascinating in many respects because he's a Jedi, one of what they call the Lost 20. Just playing a Jedi in and of itself is a unique experience, I would say, for any actor because very few are alive in the *Star Wars* world at the time. Dooku is also an antagonist—a Sith Lord. And there aren't many of them either. Being a Sith suggests that he has immense powers, both physical and mental, and that he's unstoppable.

During your career, you've dabbled a little bit in science fiction, although Star Wars *is more science fantasy . But has anything really come close to this?*

Many years ago, I appeared in one of the very first science-fiction television shows, *Space 1999*, opposite Martin Landau. But no, I've never done anything like this.

with each successive year, something incredible seems to happen, and technologically, you find things that make it easier for people to produce these amazing effects. When doing a film, I read the script so I know what the scene is about and I know what I'm supposed to be doing—but I don't know what it's going to look like behind, in front of, below, and above me until I see the film. And it really is mind-boggling how the (special) effects are implemented.

Because to know would be like peeking behind a magician's curtain?

It is magic, and magic can be created in many ways. It's like a magician who stands in front of an audience and says, "Look, nothing up this sleeve, nothing up that sleeve. Now, come with me into my magical world." The audience has no idea, except for perhaps a few specialists, how the effects are actually done. I don't want to know how it's done because I want the experience to be pure.

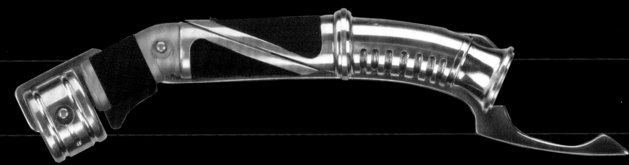

The time frame is a little bit mare far reaching as well, even more so than The Lord of the Rings*?*

I was talking with George recently about the time frame when all the events in the prequels are supposed to be happening, and he said *Star Wars* is millions of years old. *The Lord of the Rings* was only supposed to take place a mere 7,000 years ago in Middle-earth, which as far as Tolkein was concerned was somewhere near Oxford in the countryside.

The movies you've recently starred in have been very CGI intensive. What has been your experience working primarily in front of bluescreen?

I have actually done a lot of bluescreen work in my life. I've also done greenscreen and even yellowscreen at Disney. It's really all the same. But

Did you work in front of a bluescreen in the Lord of the Rings films as much as you did so for Episode II and III?

For *The Lord of the Rings*, there was a certain amount of bluescreen work to be done but nothing like this. When I saw those films, I never thought that what I was seeing was special effects—I believed it implicitly. Just as it got to the point where I didn't think of the performers as being actors and actresses dressed up playing parts, I believed them to be real people. I can also suspend this belief—or if you like, disbelief—while watching *Star Wars*. The people become real. And to the audience, they should be. After all, *Star Wars* is the ultimate in filmmaking and film viewing for literally millions of people the world over.

And that really is the testament to George Lucas' overall vision for his films.

This has all come from his head. It's not from books or stories—he's done it. Even *The Lord of the Rings* films come from three books. During filming, I had some relatives visit me on set, of which there were three children. I explained to them, the best that I could, about all the cameras, monitors, and things that were around, and they were completely bowled over.

What have you noticed about Ewan McGregor and Hayden Christensen as you've worked with them over the course of the two films?

It's been fascinating for me because I can see within minutes if they really care about what they're doing, if they really want to make it believable, and if they are dedicated to what they're doing and devoted to their craft. Ewan

has already done quite a few major films and starred in different roles. He's had a lot of good fortune. What I noticed about him is he is completely involved with everything he does—he goes straight into projects and becomes completely dedicated. That's what [acting] is all about: dedication and devotion to what you're doing. You also have to have powers of invention, you have to be imaginative, and you have to have the right instincts.

Hayden is at the beginning of his career, and when I spoke to him recently, we were talking about what an actor does these days. I told him to forget about being rich and famous and concentrate on making your own decisions (about future projects). He knows that [the *Star Wars*] films are going to make him a big name and grant him a huge following. And for a while, he knows he's going to have to live with the fact that he will be known for his role as Anakin Skywalker/Darth Vader. But I told him he's a good enough actor and that he cares enough to learn to play other roles.

Both Count Dooku and Anakin are Jedi who have or will convert to the Stith. How does Anakin's conversion differ from Dooku's.
[Dooku] crossed over for personal reasons and became a Separatist because he was disgusted with the way the Republic was functioning. But Dooku makes the switch on his own accord—nobody makes him do it, no one suggests that he do it, which is different from Anakin. He does so without knowing it or even wanting it and becomes enmeshed in a trap by the Emperor

The corruption of Anakin is uitimate goal, and the approach is very Shakespearean.
In many ways [the *Star Wars* saga] is like a Shakespearean tragedy. It's also the same with Tolkein and *The Lord of the Rings*. Don't forget that, eventually, good triumphs over evil in the end, and it follows the same course here at the conclusion of *Return of the Jedi*.

Ther's also that lust for power
Yes, and it initially emanates from the Emperor, who is also very corrupt himself. What was he like when he was a young man? Who knows? Because not many people are corrupt from the moment they're born—it does take time.

Would you say that, like the Emperor, Count Dooku is an evil character—a dad guy?
No, he's not simply a bad guy. He was good and then becomes bad. At one time, Dooku was a decent and good man. He obviously holds very strong beliefs. And maybe at one time he was right—maybe the Republic was corrupt and he decided he didn't want to become corrupt himself. So he said, "I'm going over here and I'm going to start my own group." Then, of course, it becomes a war, which is another matter altogether. Everyone has a dark side—everyone. The important thing is to make sure the dark side doesn't overpower the light side. ☮

STAR WARS LIBRARY

STAR WARS: THE MANDALORIAN GUIDE TO SEASON ONE

STAR WARS: THE MANDALORIAN GUIDE TO SEASON TWO

STAR WRS INSIDER PRESENTS THE MANDALORIANS

STAR WARS THE HIGH REPUBLIC STARLIGHT STORIES

STAR WARS THE HIGH REPUBLIC TALES OF ENLIGHTENMENT

STAR WARS: THE RETURN OF THE JEDI 40TH ANNIVERSARY SPECIAL

STAR WARS: THE PHANTOM MENACE 25TH ANNIVERSARY SPECIAL

- *ROGUE ONE: A STAR WARS STORY* THE OFFICIAL COLLECTOR'S EDITION
- *ROGUE ONE: A STAR WARS STORY* THE OFFICIAL MISSION DEBRIEF
- *STAR WARS: THE LAST JEDI* THE OFFICIAL COLLECTOR'S EDITION
- *STAR WARS: THE LAST JEDI* THE OFFICIAL MOVIE COMPANION
- *STAR WARS: THE LAST JEDI* THE ULTIMATE GUIDE
- *SOLO: A STAR WARS STORY* THE OFFICIAL COLLECTOR'S EDITION
- *SOLO: A STAR WARS STORY* THE ULTIMATE GUIDE
- *THE BEST OF STAR WARS INSIDER* VOLUME 1
- *THE BEST OF STAR WARS INSIDER* VOLUME 2
- *THE BEST OF STAR WARS INSIDER* VOLUME 3

- *THE BEST OF STAR WARS INSIDER* VOLUME 4
- *STAR WARS:* LORDS OF THE SITH
- *STAR WARS:* HEROES OF THE FORCE
- *STAR WARS:* ICONS OF THE GALAXY
- *STAR WARS:* THE SAGA BEGINS
- *STAR WARS* THE ORIGINAL TRILOGY
- *STAR WARS:* ROGUES, SCOUNDRELS AND BOUNTY HUNTERS
- *STAR WARS:* CREATURES, ALIENS, AND DROIDS
- *STAR WARS: THE RISE OF SKYWALKER* THE OFFICIAL COLLECTOR'S EDITION

- *STAR WARS: THE MANDALORIAN:* GUIDE TO SEASON ONE
- *STAR WARS: THE MANDALORIAN:* GUIDE TO SEASON TWO
- *STAR WARS: THE EMPIRE STRIKES BACK* THE 40TH ANNIVERSARY SPECIAL EDITION
- *STAR WARS: AGE OF RESISTANCE* THE OFFICIAL COLLECTORS' EDITION
- *STAR WARS: THE SKYWALKER SAGA* THE OFFICIAL COLLECTOR'S EDITION
- *STAR WARS INSIDER: FICTION COLLECTION* VOLUME 1
- *STAR WARS INSIDER: FICTION COLLECTION* VOLUME 2
- *STAR WARS INSIDER PRESENTS: MANDALORIAN SEASON 2* VOLUME 1
- *STAR WARS INSIDER PRESENTS: MANDALORIAN SEASON 2* VOLUME 2

MARVEL STUDIOS LIBRARY

MOVIE SPECIALS
- MARVEL STUDIOS' *SPIDER-MAN FAR FROM HOME*
- MARVEL STUDIOS' *ANT-MAN AND THE WASP*
- MARVEL STUDIOS' *AVENGERS: ENDGAME*
- MARVEL STUDIOS' *AVENGERS: INFINITY WAR*
- MARVEL STUDIOS' *BLACK PANTHER* (COMPANION)
- MARVEL STUDIOS' *BLACK WIDOW*
- MARVEL STUDIOS' *CAPTAIN MARVEL*
- MARVEL STUDIOS' *THE FIRST TEN YEARS*
- MARVEL STUDIOS' *THOR: RAGNAROK*
- MARVEL STUDIOS' *AVENGERS: AN INSIDER'S GUIDE TO THE AVENGERS' FILMS*
- MARVEL STUDIOS' *WANDAVISION*
- MARVEL STUDIOS' *THE FALCON AND THE WINTER SOLDIER*
- MARVEL STUDIOS' *LOKI*
- MARVEL STUDIOS' *ETERNALS*
- MARVEL STUDIOS' *HAWKEYE*
- MARVEL STUDIOS' *SPIDER-MAN: NO WAY HOME*

MARVEL STUDIOS' DOCTOR STRANGE IN THE MULTIVERSE OF MADNESS THE OFFICIAL MOVIE SPECIAL

MARVEL STUDIOS' PANTHER WAKANDA FOREVER THE OFFICIAL MOVIE SPECIAL

MARVEL STUDIOS' THOR: LOVE AND THUNDER THE OFFICIAL MOVIE SPECIAL

SPIDER-MAN ACROSS THE SPIDER-VERSE THE OFFICIAL MOVIE SPECIAL

MARVEL LEGACY LIBRARY

MARVEL'S *CAPTAIN AMERICA:* THE FIRST 80 YEARS

MARVEL: THE FIRST 80 YEARS

MARVEL'S *DEADPOOL:* THE FIRST 60 YEARS

MARVEL'S *FANTASTIC FOUR:* THE FIRST 60 YEARS

MARVEL'S *SPIDER-MAN:* THE FIRST 60 YEARS

MARVEL'S *HULK:* THE FIRST 60 YEARS

MARVEL'S *AVENGERS:* THE FIRST 60 YEARS

MARVEL CLASSIC NOVELS
- **WOLVERINE** WEAPON X OMNIBUS
- **SPIDER-MAN** THE DARKEST HOURS OMNIBUS
- **SPIDER-MAN** THE VENOM FACTOR OMNIBUS
- **X-MEN AND THE AVENGERS** GAMMA QUEST OMNIBUS
- **X-MEN** MUTANT EMPIRE OMNIBUS

NOVELS
- **MARVEL'S GUARDIANS OF THE GALAXY** NO GUTS, NO GLORY
- **SPIDER-MAN MILES MORALES** WINGS OF FURY
- **MORBIUS** THE LIVING VAMPIRE: BLOOD TIES
- **ANT-MAN** NATURAL ENEMY
- **AVENGERS** EVERYBODY WANTS TO RULE THE WORLD
- **AVENGERS** INFINITY
- **BLACK PANTHER** WHO IS THE BLACK PANTHER?
- **CAPTAIN AMERICA** DARK DESIGNS
- **CAPTAIN MARVEL** LIBERATION RUN
- **CIVIL WAR**
- **DEADPOOL** PAWS
- **SPIDER-MAN** YOUNG

- **SPIDER-MAN** KRAVEN'S LAST HUNT
- **THANOS** DEATH SENTENCE
- **VENOM** LETHAL PROTECTOR
- **X-MEN** DAYS OF FUTURE PAST
- **X-MEN** THE DARK PHOENIX SAGA
- **SPIDER-MAN** HOSTILE TAKEOVER
- **BLACK PANTHER:** TALES OF WAKANDA
- **BLACK PANTHER:** PANTHER'S RAGE
- **MARVEL'S** ORIGINAL SIN
- **MARVEL'S MIDNIGHT SUNS:** INFERNAL RISING
- **GUARDIANS OF THE GALAXY** - ANNIHILATION: CONQUEST
- **MARVEL'S** SECRET INVASION
- **CAPTAIN MARVEL:** SHADOW CODE
- **LOKI:** JOURNEY INTO MYSTERY
- **DOCTOR STRANGE:** DIMENSION WAR

ART BOOKS
- **MARVEL'S** *GUARDIANS OF THE GALAXY:* THE ART OF THE GAME
- **MARVEL'S** *AVENGERS: BLACK PANTHER:* WAR FOR WAKANDA EXPANSION: ART OF THE HIDDEN KINGDOM
- **MARVEL'S** *SPIDER-MAN: MILES MORALES* – THE ART OF THE GAME

- **MARVEL STUDIOS' THE INFINITY SAGA** - *THE AVENGERS:* THE ART OF THE MOVIE
- **MARVEL'S** *SPIDER-MAN* THE ART OF THE GAME
- **MARVEL** *CONTEST OF CHAMPIONS* THE ART OF THE BATTLEREALM
- **SPIDER-MAN: INTO THE SPIDER-VERSE** THE ART OF THE MOVIE
- **MARVEL STUDIOS' THE INFINITY SAGA** - *IRON MAN:* THE ART OF THE MOVIE
- **MARVEL STUDIOS' THE INFINITY SAGA** - *IRON MAN 2:* THE ART OF THE MOVIE
- **MARVEL STUDIOS' THE INFINITY SAGA** - *IRON MAN 3:* THE ART OF THE MOVIE
- **MARVEL STUDIOS' THE INFINITY SAGA** - *CAPTAIN AMERICA: THE WINTER SOLDIER:* THE ART OF THE MOVIE
- **MARVEL STUDIOS' THE INFINITY SAGA** - *THOR:* THE ART OF THE MOVIE
- **MARVEL STUDIOS' THE INFINITY SAGA** - *THOR: THE DARK WORLD:* THE ART OF THE MOVIE
- **MARVEL STUDIOS' THE INFINITY SAGA** - *CAPTAIN AMERICA: THE FIRST AVENGER:* THE ART OF THE MOVIE